1939

1939
Countdown to War

RICHARD OVERY

VIKING

VIKING
Published by the Penguin Group
Penguin Group (USA) Inc., 375 Hudson Street,
New York, New York 10014, U.S.A.
Penguin Group (Canada), 90 Eglinton Avenue East, Suite 700,
Toronto, Ontario, Canada M4P 2Y3
(a division of Pearson Penguin Canada Inc.)
Penguin Books Ltd, 80 Strand, London WC2R 0RL, England
Penguin Ireland, 25 St. Stephen's Green, Dublin 2, Ireland
(a division of Penguin Books Ltd)
Penguin Books Australia Ltd, 250 Camberwell Road, Camberwell,
Victoria 3124, Australia
(a division of Pearson Australia Group Pty Ltd)
Penguin Books India Pvt Ltd, 11 Community Centre, Panchsheel Park,
New Delhi – 110 017, India
Penguin Group (NZ), 67 Apollo Drive, Rosedale, North Shore 0632,
New Zealand (a division of Pearson New Zealand Ltd)
Penguin Books (South Africa) (Pty) Ltd, 24 Sturdee Avenue,
Rosebank, Johannesburg 2196, South Africa

Penguin Books Ltd, Registered Offices:
80 Strand, London WC2R 0RL, England

First American edition
Published in 2010 by Viking Penguin,
a member of Penguin Group (USA) Inc.

1 3 5 7 9 10 8 6 4 2

LIBRARY OF CONGRESS CATALOGING IN PUBLICATION DATA

Overy, R. J.
1939 : countdown to war / Richard Overy.
p. cm.
Includes bibliographical references.
ISBN 978-0-670-02209-0
1. World War, 1939–1945–Causes. 2. Europe–History–1918–1945. 3. Europe–Politics and
government–1918–1945. I. Title.
D741.O83 2010
940.53'11–dc22
2010004716

Printed in the United States of America

Contents

Preface

Every decade since the end of the Second World War has given an opportunity to reflect again on the extraordinary circumstances that led to a war of exceptional scale and destructiveness, which dwarfed even the sacrifices and losses of the Great War that preceded it. It has been tempting to think of very large causes for such a monumental conflict, and no doubt there were systemic weaknesses in the post-war world order or the capitalist system or the national geography of Europe that nourished future conflict. There was also a pervasive sense of doom that hung over the continent as it battled to come to terms with the stark reality that the region which prided itself on being at the heart of modern civilization could apparently descend into the depths of a new barbarism.

It is against this background that the present small book is set. The purpose is to tell a brief but powerful story that comes at the very end of the twenty years of insecurity and crisis that followed the Great War. However large or long-term the forces making for war, there was a moment when those forces had to be confronted and harsh decisions taken by the principal historical actors involved. In the story of those dramatic days immediately before the outbreak of war, much still stood in the balance. Great events generate their own dynamic and their own internal history. The outbreak of war now seems a natural consequence of the international crisis provoked principally by Hitler's Germany. What follows is intended to show that nothing in history is inevitable. The strange dialogue between system and actors is at the heart of historical narrative. Events themselves can be both cause and consequence, none more so than the events that led Europe to war seventy years ago.

Richard Overy
March 2009

Acknowledgements

I am grateful to a number of people for advice and help in the writing of the book, particularly to Claudia Baldoli, Lindsey Dodd, Andrew Knapp, Martin Thomas, Richard Toye, Marc Wiggam and Larysa Zariczniak. My editor, Simon Winder, never seems to tire of reading what I write and is always generous with his support; my agent Gill Coleridge was more responsible for seeing this book into print than perhaps for any of my other books, and my thanks again. What the book says is, as ever, my own responsibility.

Quotations from Vera Brittain are included by permission of Mark Bostridge and Timothy Brittain-Catlin, literary executors for the Vera Brittain Estate, 1970.

1939

Prologue

Poland, Germany and the West

In 1933 the English novelist H. G. Wells published *The Shape of Things to Come*, a fictional account of the next fifty years of world affairs. His central prediction was the coming of a 'Last War' in Europe in the near future. His chosen date was January 1940 and the cause of the new war a petty incident in Danzig, in which a Polish–Jewish commercial traveller at the main station is shot dead by a young National Socialist who has interpreted the Pole's grotesque efforts to adjust a broken dental plate as an act of mockery towards a representative of the Third Reich. In Wells' story the incident is only the spark needed to light the powder-keg of European rivalries and distrust. Within two days, war engulfs the whole of Europe. 'The tension,' Wells suggested, 'had risen to such a point at which disaster seemed like relief and Europe was free to tear itself to fragments.'[1]

Something very like this happened in the autumn of 1939, some four months earlier than Wells had predicted. European war broke out within three days of the German seizure of Danzig. Demands for the return of the formerly

German city triggered a conflict that began with a German invasion of Poland on 1 September 1939 and became a world war when the British and French empires declared war on Germany two days later. The formal cause of the conflict masked the reality that the European order was in a state of extraordinary tension by 1939, provoked by the collapse of the international system established at the end of the Great War. The conflict in September 1939 which launched the Second World War was the result of greater causes than the status of Danzig. The British prime minister, Neville Chamberlain, told the House of Commons on 24 August that war if it came would not be 'for the political future of a far away city in a foreign land', but would be fought to preserve fundamental principles of the rule of international law.[2] Adolf Hitler told his military commanders during a conference called on 23 May 1939 to prepare for war against Poland that it was not Danzig that was at stake: 'For us it is a matter of expanding our living space [*Lebensraum*] in the East and making food supplies secure.'[3]

The war that broke out in September 1939 can only be properly explained in the context of the deteriorating European order during the 1930s, when economic crisis, the rise of authoritarian dictatorships, deep ideological divisions, nationalist rivalries and the collapse of the efforts of the League of Nations to preserve peace all combined to make a major conflict probable. It was nevertheless a war ostensibly fought over the independence of Poland, and it is here, in the confrontation over Poland's future in 1939, that the immediate causes are to be found.

Above all it was Poland's intransigent refusal to make any concessions to its powerful German neighbour that made war almost certain. Poland was, wrote a British Foreign Office official in May 1939, the only state in Europe 'able and willing to offer serious resistance to German aggression'.[4]

The Polish question went back to the period immediately after the First World War when the victorious Allied powers decided to create an independent Polish state and to grant it a land corridor to the sea through former German territory, with the prospect of using the German city of Danzig as a major port for the Polish import/export trade. The port was granted status as a Free City under a League of Nations committee which was to appoint a League Commissioner to supervise the arrangements made to protect Polish trade and to preserve the principle of self-government for the largely German population.[5] The solution was never accepted on the German side, while Polish leaders recognized that the outcome was bound to provoke a future crisis of some kind. The status of the Free City, remarked Marshal Jóseph Pilsudski, ruler of Poland from 1926 until his death in 1935, would always be 'the barometer of Polish–German relations'.[6] In May 1933, shortly after Adolf Hitler came to power in Germany, Danzig's National Socialist Party won 38 out of the city's 72 assembly seats and formed the city government. From then until the outbreak of war in September 1939 Danzig was effectively an outpost of the Third Reich. By 1936 there was a virtual one-party system, and in November 1938 the city assembly, in defiance of the League Commissioner, introduced the notorious German Nuremberg Laws of 1935 to deny full citizenship to Danzig's Jewish population.[7] The strongly nationalist German population agitated in 1939 to come '*Heim ins Reich*', back home to Germany.

There was more to the Polish question than simply Danzig. In the aftermath of the Treaty of Versailles, signed in June 1919, Poland was awarded not only the Corridor through West Prussian territory but important parts of the industrial region of Silesia. German volunteer forces (*Freikorps*), recruited from among returning soldiers in 1919, fought against Polish claims along the eastern frontier until the corps were finally disbanded in 1922. The new Polish state also comprised a large area of territory that had belonged to the former Russian Empire, and in 1920 the revolutionary Red Army, fresh from victories in the Russian Civil War, invaded Poland in an attempt to destroy the infant state and spread the proletarian revolution further into Europe. Red cavalry reached almost as far as the German frontier, while Mikhail Tukhachevsky's poorly armed troops threatened to encircle Warsaw, the former capital of Russian Poland. In the absence of any effort by Britain and France to protect the state they had recently constituted, the Poles organized a remarkable victory under the leadership of Jóseph Pilsudski, who in 1914 had raised a Polish legion to fight at theside of Austria-Hungary against Tsarist Russia. The battle for Warsaw has seldom been given the weight it deserves in historical narratives of the 1920s, but it did save Eastern Europe from a communist crusade and it

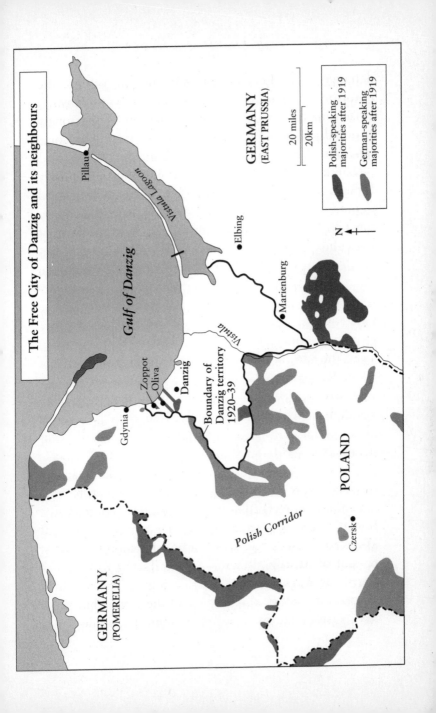

The Free City of Danzig and its neighbours

preserved the independence of Poland against its two dangerous neighbours, Germany and the Soviet Union. Victory in 1920 also became the founding myth of the new Polish state and played its part in its later determination not to be subjected to either powerful neighbour in 1939.[8]

During the inter-war years Poland maintained its fragile independence and became a significant regional power in Eastern Europe; some Polish leaders looked forward to an expansion of Polish influence towards the Black Sea or into Soviet Ukraine. In 1932 Poland signed a non-aggression pact with the Soviet Union and in 1934 signed a similar agreement with Hitler's Germany. Poland was heavily armed by the standards of Europe's smaller powers, devoting by the mid 1930s around half of government expenditure to the military. Poland was not regarded by the major Western states as a potential ally. Polish anti-Semitism and the authoritarian nature of the regime did not help in building bridges to the West. In the summer of 1938 Polish leaders were in favour of the break-up of the Czech state in the hope that Poland could dominate an independent Slovakia and become a major influence from the Baltic states to the borders of Romania. The Polish government shared in the spoils of the dismembered Czechoslovak state by issuing a successful ultimatum to the Czechs to cede the Teschen territory to Poland. It seemed to the West not unlikely that the Poles would join the German camp.[9]

The sharp deterioration of German–Polish relations to the point where Germany launched war in September

1939 resulted from the fact that Polish leaders did *not* regard Poland as part of the German camp. There was little evident tension between Poland and Germany before Munich, although the status of Danzig and the future of the Polish Corridor were elements of the postwar settlement that German leaders would have liked to resolve. The revival of German power under Hitler represented a profound threat, but Poland's leaders were determined that in their case the integrity of the Versailles settlement would be defended at all costs. Although keen to profit from the collapse of Czech resistance in 1938, Poland did not want the Munich solution to be applied to the German minorities living in Polish territory or the Free City. On the German side, the dismemberment of Czechoslovakia opened the way to further revision of the status quo in Eastern Europe. On 1 October 1938, as German troops entered the Sudeten German areas ceded in the Munich Agreement, Hitler told his army adjutant that the Polish issues had not been forgotten: 'At the given moment, when they were softened up, he would shoot the Poles.'[10] It is unlikely that at this stage Hitler thought of war with Poland. The preferred solution was agreement from Warsaw to revise the frontiers, to accept the cession of Danzig to Germany and to become part of a pro-German bloc in Eastern Europe. On 24 October 1938 the German foreign minister, Joachim von Ribbentrop, invited the Polish ambassador, Józef Lipski, to a lunch in the Grand Hotel in Berchtesgaden, close to Hitler's retreat on the Obersalzberg. Here he made the first suggestion that Danzig should be returned to Germany and a road-rail link be established across the Corridor with extra-territorial rights for Germany over the route. Poland, Ribbentrop hinted, could also align itself with Germany, Italy and Japan in the Anti-Comintern pact directed against the Soviet Union.[11]

Lipski returned to Warsaw and communicated the German suggestions to the foreign minister, Józef Beck. He was the dominant figure in the Polish government and had been at the Polish Foreign Office since 1932. Beck sensed that the German leadership was about to embark on a 'war of nerves' over Danzig. Late in November Beck made it clear to Ribbentrop that there was no question that Danzig could be reincorporated into Germany; instead he proposed an end to the League committee and a joint Polish – German agreement, respecting the interests of the two peoples in Danzig but retaining its independent status. On 24 November Hitler instructed the German armed forces to prepare a plan for the seizure of Danzig by force. On 5 January 1939 Beck was invited to Berlin, where Hitler reiterated the view that Danzig must become German. By the spring the German tone became more peremptory. On 20 March Ribbentrop told Lipski that Danzig must be returned to Germany and extra-territorial communications established. He insisted that Beck come to Berlin to negotiate.[12] The demand came during a frenetic week, only six days after the Czech president was forced to travel to Berlin to ask for 'protection' (followed by German occupation of the Czech provinces of Bohemia and Moravia) and two days before Lithuania was compelled to hand back another German territory, Memel, to German rule. Beck drew the obvious conclusion and refused to come. This was the end of friendly negotiation. Ambassador Lipski did not meet either Hitler or Ribbentrop again until 31 August, the day before the German invasion of his country. At a meeting at the Polish Foreign Office on 24 March Beck sketched out Polish options to his staff. Germany, he argued, 'had lost its calculability'. Hitler needed to be confronted with the kind of determination he had not yet encountered anywhere in Europe. Poland, Beck continued, had a baseline in negotiation below which it could not go. 'This is clear,' he continued, 'we will fight.'[13]

The battle lines of the war were laid in the last week of March 1939. On the day following Beck's meeting Hitler ordered the German armed forces to prepare an operational plan for the invasion of Poland if the Poles could be isolated internationally and if they refused to accept German demands. Polish forces on the western frontier were placed on alert that same week. In Britain, where the German occupation and break-up of Czechoslovakia had ended any illusions that Hitler could be restrained within a framework acceptable to British and French interests, the German annexation of Memel provoked growing fears that a sudden coup would add Danzig to German gains. Intelligence sent to London from Poland indicated a hardening of Polish attitudes. On 27 March the Polish Chef de Cabinet indicated that Poland would fight over Danzig. Polish opinion was, he believed, 'unprepared for even reasonable discussions'; the army was 'equally die-hard'. Secret sources indicated to the

British that Germany was about to occupy Danzig by a surprise coup. Chamberlain was informed, 'Action imminent'. [14] On 31 March in the House of Commons, Chamberlain announced a guarantee of Polish independence which was also agreed by the French government a few days later. No coup materialized, and the British assumed that Polish military mobilization and the guarantee had forced Hitler to step back, a view that encouraged greater firmness in British policy over the summer months. But Danzig was no longer regarded by anyone as the issue. Lord Halifax, the British Foreign Secretary, wrote a paper on the Danzig question for the cabinet on 5 May 1939 making clear that the problem was now one of German ambitions to dominate Europe on the one hand and Polish determination to defend their independence on the other. Although the path to a freely negotiated settlement of Danzig was still open, a compromise was now, he thought, 'unlikely'. [15]

All the sides eventually involved in the crisis in August and September that led to world war were locked into a collision course from the spring of 1939. Poland was determined not to concede to German demands, and was armed with an international guarantee to strengthen that determination. On 3 April, in reaction to the guarantee, Hitler had finally ordered preparations for 'Case White' (the invasion of Poland), to be completed by 1 September. He was determined to ensure that over the summer a wedge be driven between Poland and the Western states to make sure that war with Poland did not spread. On 23 May he told his military chiefs, 'The task is to isolate

Poland. The success of isolation is decisive . . . It must not come to a simultaneous confrontation with the West.'[16] The belief that when it came to a test of will the West would give way dominated Hitler's thinking down to the outbreak of the conflict. For their part, the British and French governments, although far from unanimous on the issue of waging a European war, made clear their position publicly again and again during the summer of 1939: if Germany acted unilaterally over Poland they would honour the guarantee to come to Poland's support. It was hoped that evidence of Western firmness would now act to deter Hitler, or force him to negotiate without threats. This hope, slim though it now seems, was also a visible thread through the crisis that ran down to war. Both sides snatched at intelligence that seemed to support the idea that the other would, at the last moment, give way.

Nevertheless in each state war preparations gathered pace in case the worst happened. Conscription was introduced in Britain in April 1939, and Anglo-French staff talks were initiated in March with a view to waging a three-year war against Germany. The Western states were not enthusiastic about Poland as an ally, but the real target of Western policy was to deter or restrain further German action in any part of Europe and to use Poland as their sticking point. The talks between Britain and France finally resulted in a plan in which an independent Poland would only be reconstituted after the end of prolonged hostilities, consigning the Poles to an early defeat.[17] When Polish leaders applied to Britain and

France for financial help with their prospective war effort, the pleas fell on deaf ears. Beck asked for a loan at the end of April to allow Poland to buy raw materials and weapons and in May a figure of £60 million was suggested. Other sums were requested in Paris, where there was initially more interest in supplying credits. The British Chancellor of the Exchequer, Sir John Simon, told Chamberlain that the idea of bailing out Polish rearmament was 'really impossible', since Britain's own financial position was weakened by heavy military spending. The British government was prepared to offer around one tenth of the sum requested, but not until 24 July was the concession made, and only if the £8 million offered were spent on British goods.[18] British reluctance infected the French, who also held back on financial help. Poland was left to fend for itself.

Although Hitler doubted Western resolve, it was clear by August 1939 that the Polish question was unlikely to be settled in Germany's favour without a crisis more profound than that generated the previous year over Czechoslovakia. To be certain of isolating Poland, Hitler authorized approaches to the Soviet Union, whose position over the Polish crisis was uncertain. Britain and France also made approaches to Stalin in the hope that a renewed entente between the three states would be sufficient to deter Hitler once and for all. Neither Western state made serious or successful attempts to cement a military or political agreement with the Soviet Union and neither could persuade Poland to co-operate, since the Polish government rightly suspected Soviet goodwill and would not accept Soviet troops on Polish soil. This failure has been regarded ever since as the greatest lost opportunity of the pre-war years. The pacifist French foreign minister, Georges Bonnet, later blamed Beck's 'incomprehensible, arrogant and treacherous attitude' for destroying the chance of the Soviet alliance. Lord Halifax, reflecting on the issue in an unpublished wartime article, understood the problem more clearly: 'An intelligent rabbit,' he wrote, 'would hardly be expected to welcome the protection of an animal ten times its size, whom it credited with the habits of a boa constrictor'.[19] From Poland's point of view, the price of Soviet co-operation might well have been as expensive as the failure to secure it at all.

In the end Stalin was more attracted to the idea of neutrality in any European conflict and the prospect of securing Soviet control over territories in Eastern Europe, so he agreed to a pact with Hitler's Germany. Although it has been argued that Stalin was forced to make a pact he did not want, not least by historians who see Soviet commitment to some form of collective security as a genuine desire to co-operate with the West, the evidence is overwhelming that the Soviet leadership played with the idea of a Western alliance in order to pressure Germany into making an agreement that gave real concessions to the Soviet side. Neither state regarded Poland as a permanent political fixture. Polish territory had been divided between Germans and Russians since the eighteenth century and the new state was only twenty years old. Destroying Poland was an acceptable outcome to both sides. The subsequent story of Ribbentrop's dramatic flight to Moscow on 22 August is well known. The resulting non-aggression pact, signed in the early morning of 24 August, and the secret protocol dividing Poland and the Baltic states into spheres of influence was greeted by Hitler as a diplomatic triumph of profound significance. He expected to hear imminently of the fall of the British and French governments. The absence of a Soviet threat added strength to his conviction that the West would not fight for Poland. 'Our enemies,' he told his commanders in a conference on 22 August, 'are tiny little worms. I saw them at Munich.'[20]

It is worth asking: who wanted war in 1939? Most Europeans certainly did not. Hitler certainly did, because he wanted to avoid any impression of weakness on his part once he had decided to prepare for the Polish invasion. He was very aware that over Munich he had been frustrated in his search for a little war against the Czechs; in front of his military chiefs he had been compelled to compromise. But he wanted war on his own terms, preferably a local war with Poland. Ribbentrop echoed his master's voice, blaming the Poles for their intransigence and threatening every kind of war. In a conversation on 12 June 1939 with the League commissioner for Danzig, the Swiss historian Carl Burckhardt, Ribbentrop reportedly said that Poland would be defeated in three days, France if it intervened 'would be reduced to the status of a third-class power', and if Britain followed suit, 'the British Empire would be smashed', while Germany would fight 'to the last woman and the last child'. It is not easy to judge what Western leaders made of such wild threats when Burckhardt passed them on a few days later, as Ribbentrop had expected he would. The record of the conversation was shown to Chamberlain, who wrote in the margin of the document that he found it 'hard to arrive at any conclusion' on the basis of such a rant.[21]

Neville Chamberlain is often painted as a man who searched for any way of evading conflict in 1939, but though he always thought peace preferable to war, he had few illusions about Hitler by the beginning of 1939. In March he described Hitler to a guest as 'the blackest devil he had ever met'.[22] He did not want war, but he recognized its strong possibility and, together with much of the British public, was ready to accept its necessity if Hitler would not see sense. The French prime minister, Édouard Daladier, and most of the French population also shared this fatalistic view. In neither case can it be demonstrated that they ever contemplated abandoning Poland if Germany acted as the aggressor. But in Poland, where tension between Poles and ethnic Germans reached an inflamed level during the summer of 1939, a serious alternative to fighting seems never to have been considered. When the British general Sir Edmund Ironside visited Poland in July 1939 to inspect its fighting power and plans, he reported an army leadership 'full of confidence', shored up by their shared memories of having defeated the Red Army as younger men in 1920. Ironside reported that 'the whole nation has made up its mind to fight', an attitude he attributed to a 'mad spirit of optimism' among the Polish people.[23] The Polish ambassador in Washington told American leaders that Polish cavalry would carry the war onto German soil 'with a reasonable prospect of success'.[24] The American journalist William Shirer, visiting the Polish port of Gdynia in August 1939, found ordinary dock workers geared up for the conflict: 'We're ready,' they told him. 'We will fight.'[25]

All this suggests that war in September 1939 was inevitable, and there were many Europeans at the time who believed that it was. There was certainly room for negotiation on the status of Danzig, which the Poles and their allies left open as long as the German leadership would accept an equal negotiation, without menaces. But for war to be avoided one of three things had to happen: Hitler had to back down again from war, as he had done at Munich, and accept an internationally agreed settlement of Polish–German disputes; or Polish leaders had to accept that war with Germany was an irrational option and agree to revise the status of Danzig and the western frontier with Germany; or British and French leaders, either in concert or alone, had to abandon the guarantee and extend to Germany an effective free hand in Eastern Europe. Although none of these positions was likely, they were possibilities. The resolve of all parties to the conflict was tested to the extreme in the extraordinary ten days of drama that separated the conclusion of the German–Soviet pact early in the morning of 24 August and the late afternoon of 3 September when France joined Britain in declaring war on Germany. The final outbreak of war was sealed by decisions taken under the immense strain of knowing that Europe risked being plunged once again into a conflict that many feared would mean the eclipse of European civilization. In the end, resolving the crisis fell to the lot of a handful of men compelled, whether they liked it or not, to act out a drama that involved the lives of millions of ordinary Europeans.

Time Running Out

24–26 August 1939

War should have broken out on the morning of 26 August with a German invasion of Poland. Hitler had ordered continuous mobilization preparations throughout August, to be kept as secret as possible. He insisted that civilian mobilization measures should not yet be put into operation, and no formal legal state of war preparation was declared. On 24 August, following the success of the negotiations with the Soviet Union, he ordered an attack to begin on the morning of 26 August. The first German formations had been moving towards the Polish frontier since 19 August and were in place four days later under code letter 'A'. The transfer of the second wave of mobilized formations, codenamed 'Y movement', began on the evening of 24 August, once the date of attack had been confirmed. Weapons and regular soldiers and SS men were smuggled into Danzig so that the city could be seized at the start of operations.[1] German forces moved into position some kilometres from the frontier, while others waited in depots and barracks with their kitbags packed for the order to move, a total of 1.5 million men. On the other side of the German–Polish frontier, mobilization also continued as inconspicuously as possible to avoid unnecessary provocation. On 23 August what amounted to a general mobilization was ordered for all army units in the Polish Corridor, Upper Silesia and much of western Poland. The air force, anti-aircraft defences and all senior staff units were also mobilized. Yet if German forces had attacked on 26 August, Poland's defences would have been even less effectively prepared than they proved to be a week later.[2]

Hitler hoped to seize the opportunity to launch the small war he had been denied the year before during the Czech crisis and which the German–Soviet pact now made less of a gamble. He had based himself at Berchtesgaden rather than Berlin for much of the summer. Goebbels visited him there for lunch on 24 August and found Hitler in an excellent mood. 'One must renew admiration again and again,' he wrote in his diary, 'for his strength of nerve.' Goebbels flew back to Berlin, where news had arrived that Britain would stick by its commitment to Poland. 'The war of nerves,' he wrote in his diary, 'approaches its climax . . . alarming news from everywhere.' He worked late into the night, and then spent sleepless hours in bed.[3] Hitler returned to Berlin that evening, to conduct his war from the capital. The following day he was to give the order to begin the attack on Poland. Goebbels visited again at midday on 25 August and found Hitler 'very determined and together'. Hitler told him to prepare two proclamations, one for the German people and one for the party, both to be broadcast on the radio as soon as war had begun.[4] At 3.02 in the afternoon he gave the order to march; the attack was to begin at 4.30 the following morning. But then, at 7.30 in the evening, while military formations were moving into position, he abruptly cancelled it. Desperate hours followed as the order was communicated to the whole military structure to ensure that no military action would be taken by accident the following morning. The German army command had already arrived at its new bunker headquarters at Zossen, south of Berlin, where they found only 'chaos' – no food, no typewriters, no telephones. They were alerted to the cancellation order only by 10.00 in the evening.[5] A small attack by German paratroopers did take place the following morning at the Jablonkow pass on the Slovak–Polish border, but it was assumed by the Polish side that this was another of the frontier skirmishes that had punctuated the previous weeks, and they made no effort to expel the German intruders.

If the attack had come on 26 August it is difficult to say with certainty that a general war would have broken out two or three days later, as it did in early September. It is just as difficult to be certain about why Hitler changed his mind. He was anxious to avoid any repeat of the previous year when he had been forced to abandon his war and accept an international conference. He was the armed forces' Supreme Commander, a post he had taken in February 1938 with the intention of playing the part of the German warlord seriously. The view in 1938 was that he had lost face over the Munich settlement. Yet here again, in August 1939, Hitler had hesitated. 'Adolf got cold feet,' commented one young German soldier to his companions when news of the cancellation came through.[6]

The explanation for Hitler's sudden hesitation lies in the course of events on the two days following the signing of the German–Soviet pact. Hitler had hoped that the pact would provoke a collapse of the Polish–British–French axis, allowing Germany to launch a swift, successful and localized attack on Poland to which the West could not effectively respond. The news of the German–Soviet rapprochement, however, had much less effect on British and French opinion than Hitler had expected, though it was a severe shock to the communist fellow-travellers and sympathizers who had put their faith in Stalin's protestations of collective security and now had to decide where they stood. For one thing, the intelligence services in Britain and France had already alerted both governments to the possibility of an agreement between the two ideological enemies, and although Western leaders remained sceptical, it was not a complete surprise. Detailed intelligence was sent to Paris on the evening of 21 August, and the following day the Soviet news agency, TASS, announced that Ribbentrop was to fly to Moscow that evening, for meetings with Soviet leaders on the 23 August.[7] Also known with some certainty was the date chosen for the German attack on Poland. A British agent in Germany, Group Captain Malcolm Christie, a former British air attaché, supplied regular and full reports for Sir Robert Vansittart, the retired permanent under-secretary at the Foreign Office, who in turn passed on the reports to the government. As early as June 1939 Christie relayed information that German mobilization would begin from 1 August to be completed by the 27th of the month; on 17 August Christie, whose sources included senior German officers and officials hostile to Hitler, reported that action was timetabled for any day between 25 and 28 August. This chimed with French secret intelligence from the Czech agent 'A-54', who had told the French that 26 August would be the day of invasion.[8] On 19 August Halifax sent the information to Chamberlain, who was on a fishing holiday at Lairg in Scotland. The following day Chamberlain came back to London, undecided about whether to return to his holiday a few days later.[9]

Chamberlain was not the only one forced to interrupt his holiday. Halifax returned on 19 August from Yorkshire, while the British war minister, Leslie Hore-Belisha, came back from Cannes on 22 August. King George VI came down from a shooting holiday at the royal castle at Balmoral in Scotland a day later to find that Chamberlain had already summoned parliament to meet on 24 August without asking his consent. The king was put out that excellent hunting (his party had already shot 1,600 brace of grouse) was brought to a premature halt: he 'had been much looking forward to this week's shoot', he told the British ambassador to Egypt a few days later. 'It was utterly damnable that the villain Hitler had upset everything.'[10] Chamberlain told the king that the German–Soviet pact had caused the sudden recall of parliament but that it 'made no difference to our position'. He asked the king to be prepared by the end of the following day to sign into law the Emergency Powers (Defence) Bill which would allow the government to publish the necessary

Defence Regulations with the force of law.[11] The legislation, which Chamberlain wanted to steamroller through parliament in one day, provoked immediate argument. Trade union leaders were worried that the bill could be used to outlaw strikes, introduce industrial conscription and muzzle the press, and had to be reassured by the home secretary that it would not. The Labour Party wanted a temporary measure only, which Chamberlain agreed to. The Liberal Party leaders objected to the provision in Clause 6 that traitors were to be shot rather than hanged, and Chamberlain gave way on this in the hope of getting everything through quickly.[12]

This was only one of a number of preparations for a possible war that were set in motion even before the German–Soviet pact was actually signed. Chamberlain refused to sanction a general mobilization, which the war minister and the service chiefs would have liked, because of the fear that, as in 1914, it would be used as a pretext by other states to mobilize in retaliation; but on 22–23 August the first stage of calling up 'key parties' to man staff rooms, command posts and anti-aircraft units was authorized, and on 24 August all anti-aircraft and coastal defence positions were ordered to be fully mobilized, involving more than 120,000 men.[13] The first steps were taken to prepare the membership of a War Cabinet, which, on the advice of Lord Hankey, the former cabinet secretary, should include Winston Churchill, to satisfy public expectation, but not David Lloyd George, prime minister from 1916 to 1922, whom Hankey regarded as untrustworthy.[14] Chamberlain also took the step of warning Hitler, even before the pact was certain, that it would have no effect on Britain's obligations to the Poles, which the British government 'were determined to fulfil'. He called on Germany to accept a truce in the confrontation and proper discussions between Poland and Germany. In parliament two days later Chamberlain reiterated his pledge in the face of 'the imminent peril of war' that the commitments entered into for the defence of Poland would be honoured unreservedly, 'so that no doubt might remain in the mind of the German Government'.[15] The speech was not regarded as an inspiring one ('like a coroner summing up a case of murder', commented the MP Harold Nicolson), but the mood of the House of Commons, as another MP noted, was quite different from the mood before Munich. 'Fear,' he claimed, 'had disappeared,' to be replaced by a keen vigilance 'for any sign of weakness' in the British response.[16]

In France the news of the pact was a profound disappointment, since the French government had always placed greater faith in the possibility of a Soviet alliance than had the British. But as in Britain there was a growing sense that this made war more rather than less likely. 'Almost all the politicians believe there will be war,' wrote a French Foreign Office official on 24 August. 'Those who believe that Hitler will step back grow fewer and fewer. And the intransigents accept the idea of war certainly without pleasure, but with anger.'[17] Nevertheless there remained more division within the French leadership than in Britain. The foreign minister, Georges Bonnet, an ambitious schemer recruited to the cabinet by Daladier in 1938 to prevent him from undermining his government from the backbenches, was a pacifist of deep conviction. He had fought and been wounded during the Great War, and had lost brothers in the conflict. He certainly disapproved of German diplomacy, and when required restated the commitment to Poland, but he was convinced that the pact with Poland had locked France into an obligation impossible to fulfil and wanted to find some way of avoiding it. He thought that the German–Soviet pact gave him the opportunity. At a meeting of the National Defence Council summoned on 23 August in response to the alliance, Daladier asked the heads of the three armed services whether France could now contemplate a war; to Bonnet's evident discomfiture, the chiefs of the army and navy affirmed that French military strength and preparations were equal to a war. The French air minister, rather than the more pessimistic chief of the French air force, then added that although French air power was still behind German, enough had been done to allow France to act. At a cabinet meeting the following day Bonnet argued that the circumstances had changed so much that the guarantee to Poland could no longer be honoured, even if France could contemplate war.[18] The majority of the cabinet were opposed to any second Munich, including Daladier, who had no taste for war but saw now that it was probably unavoidable unless Germany could be made to back down. Bonnet nevertheless continued for the following week to seek some way of sabotaging Western commitment to fight, while Daladier authorized the steps necessary to bring France to a state of preliminary mobilization, ordered on 24 August.

The reassertion of the commitment to Poland needs little explanation, but it has so often been suggested that Chamberlain, Halifax and Daladier were appeasers looking for a way out of their obligations that their renewed firmness requires some elaboration. It could be argued that many of the factors that inhibited a firm response in the case of the Czech crisis the year before had disappeared. Both Britain and France had accelerated their rearmament during 1939, particularly in the air. 'We can face the struggle,' General Gamelin, commander-in-chief of the French army, told Daladier in August 1939; 'we have a respectable parity in equipment.'[19] The British army chief of staff confided to his diary the view that only war would stop Hitler now: 'we must have a war. We can't lose it.'[20] The gap between Western and German military strength was much narrower than is usually allowed; by the spring of 1940 the Western allies had more men, more tanks and only marginally fewer aircraft than the Germans. A second factor was the state of public opinion, which had shifted from dread of war and a longing for peace evident in September 1938 to a fatalistic acceptance that war was now unavoidable and should be waged sooner rather than later. In both Britain and France there remained a vociferous pacifist and anti-war lobby which argued for peace at any price right up to the outbreak of war and beyond. The British MP Edward Spears, holidaying in France in August, found fear of war still creating a profound sense of apprehension among his French friends: 'Why, they asked, had the world gone mad? . . . Could not a settlement be found that would avoid war?'[21] But in France, too, opinion hardened sufficiently for Daladier to be more confident that he could take the country into war if it had to be so.

It would be wrong, nonetheless, to assume that Chamberlain, Halifax and Daladier accepted the risk of war only because they were pressured to do so by public opinion. Each in their own way had come to accept during the course of 1939 that the use of force was necessary in the face of a crumbling European order. Indeed, all three reached this point a year earlier on 28 September 1938, when war would have had to be declared if Hitler had unilaterally violated Czech sovereignty, an element of the Munich story that is readily forgotten.[22] War was perhaps hardest for Chamberlain, who was convinced when he became British prime minister in May 1937 that he could achieve a 'Grand Settlement' of world affairs by appealing to the practical self-interest of other states. He could not understand why any statesman would rather choose war than peace. In pursuing a policy of 'appeasement' he was supported by much of his government and country and did so, as one of his parliamentary colleagues put it, with a 'concentration of purpose and narrowness of vision' that alienated many of his critics.[23] He came from a traditional nineteenth-century liberal background and a career in municipal politics in Birmingham before becoming a successful minister of health and then, from 1932, chancellor of the exchequer. In an article in an American journal in November 1939, the Conservative politician Alfred Duff Cooper, a stern critic of his prime minister, observed that Chamberlain 'had never met anyone in Birmingham who in the least resembled Adolf Hitler . . . Nobody in Birmingham had ever broken his promise to the mayor.'[24] What Cooper and others failed to grasp was the deep sense of personal betrayal felt by Chamberlain when Hitler did break his word by occupying the Czech state on 15 March. From March 1939 onwards Chamberlain – described by a parliamentary colleague as 'a man not of straw, but of iron' – turned his singleness of purpose and unyielding temperament to the task of obstructing any further violence to the European order.[25] This did not exclude the possibility of a peaceful settlement, which he would have preferred, but required the dictators to make gestures of good faith which Chamberlain had no confidence they would do.

Chamberlain's foreign secretary, Edward, Lord Halifax, came to office in February 1938 after a distinguished career as a patrician imperialist and, until 1931, Viceroy of India. He was a deeply religious man who never hesitated to apply his powerful sense of Christian values to his conduct of foreign affairs. This made him a natural enemy of the values of dictatorship and, as his parliamentary secretary wrote in a private profile of his superior, inspired in him 'a strong belief in our own system of living and our own ideals'. As a result Halifax was more ready than Chamberlain to make it clear that Hitler's international behaviour could not be tolerated. In notes for a speech delivered in June 1939 he observed that the issues of war or peace dominated public debate that summer not because of narrow questions of foreign policy but because 'great issues [are] being tested vital to our way of life'. British policy, Halifax continued, was to 'throw all we can into the scales on the side of law as opposed to lawlessness in Europe'.[26] One peer listening to Halifax in the House of Lords on 24 August reaffirming commitment to Poland thought he expressed 'Too much high-fallutin principles and not enough plain patriotism and self-protection', but the issue of principle was central to Halifax's world view, and he brought it to bear consistently during the days of crisis. Like Chamberlain, he did not shut the door to the possibility of reaching agreements in good faith, but like Chamberlain he thought that good faith from Hitler was improbable.[27]

Édouard Daladier had a more difficult task than British leaders because of the crisis faced by French politics in the last years of the 1930s. A former history teacher from Provence, Daladier became a leader of the French Radical Party, a centre party despite its name, which represented a solid petty-bourgeois constituency of shopkeepers, teachers and peasants. He was a man of long ministerial experience, and under the Popular Front government – a temporary alliance of socialists, radicals and communists which came to power in May 1936 – he was appointed minister of war with responsibility for seeing through a four-year programme of accelerated rearmament. He had a reputation for great energy, which earned him the nickname 'the bull of Vaucluse', but he also suffered from chronic indecisiveness. Unkind critics dubbed him 'the bull with snail's horns'. In April 1938 the Popular Front broke up and Daladier formed a government without communist support. Continued industrial unrest and conflicts between extreme right and left inhibited the French response to the Czech crisis, but Daladier, backed by emergency powers, used decrees to stifle communist activity and force the pace of rearmament. By the summer of 1939 he had, one British observer remarked, 'almost dictatorial powers'.[28] He disliked the idea of war but thought it virtually inevitable. The British war minister, after meeting him on 21 August, noted that though Daladier saw the Poles as 'fools governed by outworn opinions of Pilsudski', he was confident that the British and French had 'superior resources' to the Germans. He hoped that Italy would also join in the contest because, he told Hore-Belisha, 'This would give us the chance of an initial military success.'[29]

The public reiteration of the Anglo-French commitment to Poland following the German–Soviet agreement was the first issue that Hitler had to confront in deciding whether to embark on war as he intended. The confrontation produced a heightened anxiety throughout Europe on the morning of 25 August. In Poland that day there was a mood of profound suspense. 'We are living in unusual tension,' wrote the Polish doctor Zygmunt Klukowski in his diary. 'I know that war will start soon. People are anxious; you can hear that everybody wants it to start now.' The beginning of the Polish school year was postponed and all holidays cancelled.[30] Sir Henry 'Chips' Channon worked all day at the Foreign Office in London 'wondering whether there would be war'. 'Every few minutes,' he continued in his diary, 'the barometer rose and fell.'[31] The same morning Vita Sackville-West wrote to the novelist Virginia Woolf about her own war psychology.

Each day until midday, she wrote, she was in a state of dread of air-raids, gas and bombs and then gradually became 'all brave and British again' until the following morning 'when the whole thing starts up again in its terrible cycle of fear, dread and shrinking cowardice'.[32] In Berlin the atmosphere appeared calmer. 'The people in the streets,' wrote William Shirer in his diary, 'are still confident Hitler will pull it off again without war.'[33] Hitler still expected war but hoped the guarantees from Britain and France would not be honoured. 'The Führer still works in the direction of a local war, which he will not abandon,' wrote Ribbentrop's state secretary in his diary. Hitler, he continued, had expected that Chamberlain's speech to parliament on the afternoon of 24 August would bring about a localization of the war. When the opposite happened, Hitler directed his energies to 'splitting off the English from the Poles' before his planned invasion of Poland.[34]

Across the Atlantic the American government also watched the unfolding events in the hope that peace at all costs could be preserved. The United States were involved little in the final crisis that led to war. Years of isolationist politics and the formal passing of neutrality legislation in 1937 ensured that whatever the outcome of the Polish crisis, America would not be drawn into war. An opinion poll in August showed that 92 per cent of Americans did not want to send forces to Europe if war came. One of President Roosevelt's policy advisers, writing in June 1939, summed up the American position thus: 'We should not endeavour to pull the chestnuts of other countries out of the fires in which those chestnuts may lie; but we must look after our own chestnuts . . .'[35] When news of the German–Soviet pact broke, Roosevelt decided to send an immediate appeal for peace to the leaders involved in the Polish crisis, but it had little effect. The German Foreign Office pretended to know nothing about it when the American *chargé d'affaires* enquired on 25 August. The German government finally sent a formal reply on 31 August, on the eve of invasion, blaming the Poles for sabotaging the prospects for a peaceable solution.[36] Roosevelt was more interested in a report circulated to the White House on 25 August that suggested Hitler only wanted to inflict a diplomatic defeat on the West, but could not face a world war. 'Very, very interesting,' Roosevelt scrawled on the report.[37] The dangers were nevertheless evident. Roosevelt's mother, visiting France, took the first available ship back to New York on 24 August; four days later Roosevelt ordered searches of European merchant ships in US ports which might be preparing to convert to some kind of military role if war broke out.[38] When Neville Chamberlain sent Roosevelt a personal letter on 25 August asking him to release the American Norden bombsight for use in British bombers, Roosevelt refused on the grounds that it would compromise American efforts to retain a strict impartiality.[39] The American government and public, however sympathetic to the Western cause, kept a clear distance between them and the sharpening European crisis.

During the morning of 25 August, Hitler continued to discuss war preparations with his military adjutants, who moved between the general staffs and the chancellery, where Hitler's supreme command staff were also temporarily based. He was ill-tempered from the reports in the British press that he wanted to conquer the world, and at 12.45 summoned Nevile Henderson, the British ambassador, to a discussion which was designed as one final effort to separate Britain from its Polish pledge. The meeting lasted an hour and was conducted with cordiality on both sides. 'The Chancellor,' wrote Henderson later, 'spoke with calm and apparent sincerity.'[40] Hitler affirmed the necessity of solving the Polish question once and for all, for the sake of European stability, but after that talked of offering Britain the hand of friendship 'as decisive as the move as regards Russia', which had resulted in an unexpected pact. He promised to guarantee the British Empire and come to its defence. The result, he concluded, might be 'a blessing for Germany and the British Empire'. This was, he said, 'his last offer'.[41] He told Henderson that he had an aircraft ready to fly him to London so that he could communicate directly with his government, but Henderson in fact flew off only the next day, by which time Hitler had planned for German troops to be fighting on Polish soil, presenting the British government, when Henderson arrived, with a difficult decision from which Hitler hoped they would back away.

After Henderson had departed, Hitler gave the order to march the following morning. He was still waiting to hear from his Axis partner, the Italian dictator Benito Mussolini, with whom he had signed a military alliance in May. That morning he had notified Mussolini that war with Poland was imminent. It is by no means clear that German leaders wanted Italy to fight at their side over Poland, but Italy was useful to Hitler's calculations as a way of putting pressure on Britain and France in the Mediterranean and reducing the chances of Western intervention. For Mussolini, German moves in the summer of 1939 were difficult to accept. When the Italian foreign minister, Mussolini's son-in-law Count Galeazzo Ciano, met Ribbentrop at Salzburg on 12 August, he was told that Germany intended to attack Poland in the near future, but that the war would be localized. 'Poland,' said Ribbentrop, 'must be defeated, annihilated, annexed.'[42] Mussolini knew that Italy was in no position to risk a war with the Western states, not only because of a clear inferiority in armaments, but also because Italian public opinion had not been prepared for it. Italy's military and financial position made neutrality essential, and it was this reason that Mussolini gave in his reply to Hitler. But Italian leaders were also alarmed by the German–Soviet pact, which had the effect of pushing Italy further away from the centre of European politics. The conference at Munich the year before saw Mussolini centre-stage; the Polish crisis pushed Italy to the fringes.[43] This did not stop Italian newspapers from hailing the German–Soviet pact as an end to the 'encirclement' of their Axis partner; 'the reconstruction of Europe,' ran one headline, 'is in the hands of the Axis powers'.[44] But the realization that Italy was left in the dark about German intentions coloured Mussolini's subsequent response.

An hour or so after Hitler had given the order for the attack on Poland, the Italian ambassador, Bernardo Attolico, who had once been the League Commissioner for Danzig, arrived at the chancellery with Mussolini's letter announcing that Italy would remain neutral. In the lobby he met Ribbentrop's state secretary, Ernst von Weizsäcker, who advised him to speak clearly to Hitler about Italian intentions. Mussolini and Ciano were on the beach, Attolico complained, and could not be reached, leaving him to convey the unpleasant news.[45] At around 5.45 Attolico was ushered in to see Hitler. He delivered the message and was then coldly dismissed. Hitler and his entourage indulged in a brief flurry of anti-Italian sentiment, and then contemplated what to do. At 5.30, shortly before Attolico's visit, the French ambassador, Robert Coulondre, had also arrived at the chancellery, and Hitler, less calm than he had been with Henderson, had reiterated his desire to have peaceful relations with France. On the point of being dismissed, Coulondre hastily retorted, on his word as a former soldier, that if Poland was attacked France would stand with its forces at Poland's side. When he tried to continue, Hitler interrupted him: 'Why, then, give a blank cheque to Poland?'[46] These were not the only uncertainties Hitler suddenly had to confront that afternoon. The Japanese ambassador had been cool as a result of the German–Soviet pact, which Japan regarded as a threat to its security in Eastern Asia. The pact itself was still not ratified by Moscow, and although it was unlikely that Stalin would change his mind, there was still the doubt that Stalin was watching to see what would happen in the crisis (in the end the pact was not ratified until 31 August).[47] Finally, at 6 p.m., after Attolico had left, Ribbentrop arrived with news of the signing earlier that afternoon in London of an Anglo-Polish treaty.

According to a German embassy official in London, who leaked the story the following day, news of the treaty arrived in Berlin as a 'bombshell'.[48] Hitler took it to be the British response to the offer he had just given to Henderson and regarded it, one witness later reported, 'as a slap in the face'.[49] Its impact was almost certainly magnified by the effect of the difficult hour Hitler had just spent with Coulondre and Attolico. In London there was some anxiety that the declaration of the treaty might make the situation worse. Richard Butler, Halifax's parliamentary secretary, advised that signature 'would have a bad psychological effect upon Hitler and would wreck the negotiations'.[50] After months of discussion and two weeks of preparation, signing on that particular day was in fact fortuitous, although Halifax must have been well aware of its implications. The Polish ambassador in London, Edouard Raczyński, arrived at the Foreign Office during the afternoon, and the Agreement of Mutual Assistance – given this title so that Poland could also come to Britain's assistance if required – was formally signed. The agreement committed each party to give all the 'support and assistance in its power' to the other if it found itself attacked by another European power. The second article of the agreement specified similar assistance where a third power 'indirectly' threatened one of the signatories, which then responded with force. This rather cryptic formulation was published in the press, excluding the more provocative Protocol to the agreement where it was stated that 'by the expression "European Power" is to be understood Germany', and by the indirect threat was meant

Danzig. If another European power attacked either of them, the protocol committed them only to consult.[51]

There was a pause of around an hour between the arrival of this news and the decision to cancel the military assault the following morning. Hitler's air adjutant, Nicolaus von Below, overheard Ribbentrop advising Hitler to stop the order and to consider all the implications of what had happened that afternoon. Goebbels noted that night in his diary, 'Every disposition must be overturned . . . everything stays temporarily in abeyance.'[52] The army commander-in-chief, General Walther von Brauchitsch, arrived to encourage Hitler to continue his 'political game' of localizing the conflict. At 7.45 an officer was sent to find the army chief of staff, while Wilhelm Keitel, chief of Hitler's supreme headquarters staff, ordered an adjutant to rescind the order to march. Hermann Göring, who was also present in the chancellery, asked if the war was cancelled or postponed. 'No,' Hitler said, 'I will have to see whether we can eliminate England's intervention.'[53] The following day mobilization continued, allowing what had been a hurried few days of deployment to be continued more carefully. Between 25 and 31 August a further twenty-one infantry divisions and two motorized divisions were in place, while armaments for other units were strengthened.[54] From 26 August all German airports were closed, and German airspace became a restricted zone. Diplomats had to apply for permission to travel outside Berlin. The wheels of war continued to turn even while the order to fight was suspended.

It is difficult to gauge Hitler's state of mind that evening when the cancellation order was given. A year before he had been ill-tempered when he had had to cancel the planned invasion of Czechoslovakia. He was observed by an adjutant to be 'irritable, grim and sharp' following the second cancellation, when he had once again very publicly held back from a war he manifestly wanted.[55] The strain of the war of nerves played on his fragile personality as much as it did on others. When Burckhardt had met him a week earlier he had seemed older and paler: 'He gave the impression of fear, and seemed nervous, pathetic and almost shaken at times.' Burckhardt suggested that the outcome in the near future would very much depend on 'Hitler's state of mind'.[56] The decision to cancel the attack perhaps reflected this constant strain, exacerbated suddenly by an accumulation of political shocks which challenged his resolve. He was a notoriously poor negotiator, as Ivone Kirkpatrick, assigned to the British embassy in the mid 1930s, told Harold Nicolson shortly before the outbreak of war:

one has such a sense of evil arrogance that one is almost nauseated . . . Evil and treachery and malice dart into Hitler's mystic eyes. He has a maddening habit of laying down the law in sharp, syncopated sentences, accompanying the conclusion either with a sharp pat of his palm upon the table, or by a half-swing sideways in his chair, a sudden Napoleonic crossing of the arms, and a gaze of detached but suffering mysticism towards the ceiling. His impatience is terrific.[57]

The crisis that emerged on 25 August owed much to Hitler's inability to understand the arts of diplomacy and political finesse, which years of political struggle had failed to teach him. On this occasion, unlike the Austrian *Anschluss* in March 1938 or the decisions that led to the Munich agreement, he did not rely on others to make the choice for him. Yet left to himself the decision seems to have been difficult to make. He recognized that a war with the West was one of the possibilities, but no sense can be made of his desperate efforts to break the Polish–Western alliance unless his preferred solution was the local war he planned for. All these imponderables proved too much on the day war should have started, but the initial hesitation then made it almost impossible for Hitler to risk humiliation in front of his military leaders by backing down again when a decision had to be made a few days later.

In the end 26 August was something of an anticlimax in Berlin. Although it was soon guessed in the West that war should have broken out that day, it does not seem to have been known on the day itself. Chamberlain, waiting to hear about the interview between Henderson and Hitler, thought the day might be 'decisive', though it is not clear why.[58] The text of Hitler's offer had already been sent through, and Halifax and Chamberlain worked on a draft reply from late at night on 25 August. Henderson flew from Berlin to Croydon airport, but then his car broke down on the way into London, and he did not arrive to see Chamberlain until 1 p.m. His oral report added little to what was already known, and the rest of the day was spent in drafting a satisfactory response first at No. 10 among a small group, then in cabinet, then at the Foreign Office late in the evening. It was not completed until 28 August. There were several reasons why such careful attention was paid to a single document: it would give Hitler no opportunity to exploit the wording to his advantage; it would show absolute commitment to the Polish treaty; and it would leave the door open if Hitler chose to abandon violence and accept a free and equal negotiation.[59] There was also some sense that Hitler's offer might seriously represent the start of a climb-down. The *Daily Telegraph* headlines read 'Fresh Talks in Berlin', 'German Demands Modified?'[60] That same day news arrived from a counsellor at the German embassy in London which gave further encouragement to the idea that Hitler might be deterred. Talking off the record to William Strang, a Foreign Office official, the counsellor said that there might now be 'hesitation in Berlin as to the course to follow' and 'the germ of a settlement' if the Poles would not fight for Danzig. Strang commented, 'I take his view to be that with absolute (but unprovocative) firmness on our part and with prudence and moderation on the part of the Poles, a peaceful way out is still just possible.'[61]

Poland in the Middle

27–31 August

The five days that separated the cancelled German attack from the German assault on Poland on the morning of Friday 1 September were coloured by a growing optimism in the West that a policy of staying firm would force Hitler to back down. The danger of war remained a grave one, but the whole of Western and Polish strategy had been predicated from earlier in the year on the idea of deterrence. Since Hitler had apparently forced himself into a corner over the confrontation with Poland, the West also left open the path to possible negotiation, not on the lines of the Munich agreement the year before, but on equal terms, without threats of violence or unilateral action.

This new direction explains the inordinate time devoted to composing a reply to Hitler's offer. The eventual letter repeated Britain's support for Poland and its determination to honour its commitment to the Anglo-Polish treaty, but it also suggested that no useful discussions about German–British understanding could take place before the Polish question had been settled by a negotiation between equal parties, guaranteed by international settlement. In the discussions in cabinet and at No. 10 every effort was made to remove any hint that Britain was weakening in support for Poland. It was decided to remove the sentence 'In the end, when all have suffered alike, it would make little difference on whose shoulders the immediate responsibility for its beginning might be held to rest.' Sir John Simon, the home secretary, commenting on the draft, observed, 'There will not be a shadow of a doubt who is *exclusively* responsible for this one.'[1] The war minister, Hore-Belisha, scribbled down notes for discussion about the letter in cabinet: 'Either bluffing or not. If "yes" we are all right. If "no" we must not compromise the position by giving anything of the Polish case away on our own.' He thought Halifax's original draft not firm enough and added to his notes, 'We are prepared for war unless he [Hitler] is prepared for negotiation *on = terms*.'[2] Almost all the alterations in the direction of greater firmness were accepted, and the final letter, despatched by plane with Nevile Henderson to Berlin on the evening of 28 August, was completed only in the afternoon. The text reflected the mood in the Foreign Office, which Richard Butler, Halifax's parliamentary secretary, described as 'an absolute inhibition not to press the Poles to negotiate', evident throughout the final days before the conflict.[3] Firmness, it was assumed, would pay dividends.

The situation in France differed only because Hitler had not considered it likely that the French government would act on its own without Britain, and focused attention on detaching the British from their commitment. In Paris, too, there surfaced a growing optimism based on regular reports from French diplomats in Germany that the failure to go to war on 26 August reflected a growing weakness on the German side. On 27 August Robert Coulondre, the French ambassador to Berlin, in Paris for discussions, insisted, according to the Foreign Office official Boyer de Sainte-Sauzanne, 'One must hold firm, Hitler faced with force is a man who will climb down.'[4] The following day there was rising optimism in Paris that 'Hitler hesitates more and more'. The chatter at the Quai D'Orsay was of a war of nerves, with Hitler struggling to find a way out of the Polish dilemma. 'German morale,' noted Boyer on 29 August, 'is yielding; ours by contrast is strengthening.' There was a mood of firmness among many French officials and ministers that matched that in London: 'In risking a red war, the war will remain white,' was the view among Boyer's colleagues.[5] Georges Bonnet interpreted the changed mood as the opportunity for a second Munich. He redoubled his efforts to encourage an Italian initiative for a conference, to persuade Warsaw to abandon Danzig and to invite interventions for peace first from Leopold III, King of the Belgians, then, improbably, from Francisco Franco, the recent victor of the Spanish Civil War.[6] Bonnet and his allies were prepared to go much further in pressuring Poland, but the French *munichois*, enthusiasts for a Munich solution, of whom Bonnet was the chief spokesman, could do so only because they too believed Hitler might be brought to the conference table rather than accept war.

Nonetheless, preparations for a possible conflict continued. In Poland, where Beck still argued that firmness in the face of German intimidation would provoke a settlement that respected Polish interests, the stages of mobilization were put in place. On 27 August the remaining Polish reserve units were mobilized, and the following day measures were taken for 'frontier clearance west', to ensure that the frontier areas were ready for military action and the population evacuated. On the morning of 29 August troops were moved into their forward positions preparatory for combat, though no general mobilization was ordered.[7] In Britain the War Office ordered the mobilization of 35,000 Territorial Army soldiers on 27 August, and the following day all 'key parties' of the main army Field Force were called up so that the army could quickly be expanded on the announcement of general mobilization, which Chamberlain still was not willing to order in case it should prove too provocative.[8] Other steps were taken that reflected the seriousness of the situation. Britain's major art treasures began the move from the galleries and museums in London. This cultural evacuation had been planned since April but was only approved in the last week of August. The Natural History Museum, the Victoria and Albert Museum and the Imperial War Museum were allocated a total of thirty-one lorries to transport the most valuable exhibits to the rural areas around London and to the west of England. The other major museums and galleries were allocated eighty-eight lorries and container vans to transport treasures to the main London railway stations, from where they were sent to a number of British stately homes to be stored.[9] The museum authorities applied for police guards, partly from fear of attacks by the Irish Republican Army, which was currently engaged in a campaign of terrorism in mainland Britain. When the police authorities refused to guarantee protection all along the route, on the grounds that the war emergency gave them more important things to do, the organizers suggested arming the museum and gallery staff, so that they could protect their valuable cargoes. This was refused and the evacuation was undertaken with the minimum of security protection and without incident.[10]

The continued preparations reflected the uncertainties of the situation, but the mood of greater optimism was not a mere delusion. During the last days of August there was a growing accumulation of evidence, much of it supplied by the secret services, to show that Germany was experiencing economic and political tensions and that Hitler's actions were dictated by a growing desperation at the situation he had created for himself. The intelligence picture was one that had formed organically over the year since the Munich settlement. It was assumed in the West that the German economy was faced with serious difficulties in financing rearmament, funding overseas trade and suppressing living standards. This argument was central to most British and French intelligence assessments of German prospects, and it became embedded in the minds of Western politicians when they sought to detect, in the final days of crisis, chinks in the German armour.[11] A second illusion, also the product of a long gestation in the intelligence service assessments of the political situation, was a growing belief that Hitler faced the prospect of a serious political threat, either from conservative opponents of his regime or from within the heart of the National Socialist Party itself. In the midst of efforts to redraft the letter to Hitler, news arrived at Downing Street from the head of the SIS, Sir Hugh Sinclair, that there was fresh evidence of dissension in the German army general staff and that Göring was working against Hitler in order to find a peaceful solution.[12] On 28 August Sinclair sent his assistant, David Boyle, to Berlin in the same plane as Henderson, to investigate the truth of these assertions. Boyle returned the following day to confirm that there were indeed divisions in the German high command, and news of this additional pressure on Hitler was passed on to the government.[13]

The assessment of possible resistance to Hitler was fuelled throughout by the conservative opposition to the dictatorship. The opposition was loosely based around the former German army chief of staff, Ludwig Beck, and the former mayor of Leipzig, Carl Goerdeler, both of whom were to pay with their lives in the aftermath of the failed July Plot to assassinate Hitler five years later. It involved a number of prominent German conservatives, including Hitler's former economics minister, Hjalmar Schacht, and the former German ambassador to Italy, Ulrich von Hassell. But there were also conservatives sympathetic to the opposition who worked closely in the state apparatus, particularly the state secretary in the German Foreign Office, Ernst von Weizsäcker, the army chief of staff, Lt. General Franz Halder, the head of German counter-intelligence, Admiral Wilhelm Canaris, and the head of the War Economy and Armaments staff at supreme headquarters, Major-General Georg Thomas. Their opposition, however, was limited and conditional.[14] In the final week of crisis this group, which constituted neither a party nor a real conspiracy, also came to hope along with Western leaders that firmness would at least open the door to negotiation, or in the best case, provoke the collapse of the Hitler regime.

The opposition hoped to achieve a solution in which war was avoided entirely. In Germany they tried to find ways to convince the regime or the military leadership that the risk of a general war was too great. General Thomas drafted a memorandum for Hitler that unfavourably (but not inaccurately) contrasted the economic and military potential of the Western powers, including the United States, with the material position of Germany. He presented it on the Sunday before the start of war, 27 August. When Hitler's chief of staff, Wilhelm Keitel, showed Hitler the memorandum he responded, Thomas later recalled, with the argument that he did not share anxiety 'over the danger of a world war' since the Soviet alliance made a local war certain.[15] Efforts were also made to impress upon Halder and the army commander-in-chief, Walther von Brauchitsch, the urgent need to

obstruct Hitler's drift to war, but both senior commanders refused to meet the doubters. When von Hassell asked
Brauchitsch's cousin on 26 August to talk to her distinguished relative, she telephoned the following day to
say that she had done so but he had just stared at her
and said nothing.[16] Schacht and other opponents also
tried to intercede directly with the army leadership on
the evening when war was cancelled, but they were
denied access to the War Ministry. Instead, one of their
allies, the counter-intelligence officer Hans Oster,
emerged from the ministry with the news that the march-
ing order was rescinded. Hans Gisevius, one of the group
waiting outside, later recalled that Oster interpreted this
decision as a major victory for peace: 'The Fuehrer is
done for,' Oster said. 'It was now merely a question of
time and manner: how could this unmasked imposter be
removed with the least trouble and the most elegance?'[17]
Over the week that followed, Gisevius wrote in his
memoirs, an apathetic mood reigned among the opposition in Berlin. 'No one was thinking of war any more,'
he wrote. 'Everyone was convinced that a week of negotiations was about to begin.'[18]

To ensure that the British and French remained firm,
the conservatives kept up their efforts to explain to their
foreign contacts the internal situation in Germany. On
27 August a friend of Goerdeler's, Reinhold Schairer,
arrived at the British Foreign Office with a message from
Goerdeler, who was in Oslo, reporting views among the
army leadership in Germany. Goerdeler noted that 'The
Rome–Berlin–Tokyo axis is completely broken' but also

that Hitler was still confident that Britain and France would not fight. The minute of the discussion with Schairer concluded: 'At all costs England and France must remain firm. If they do so Hitler will in the last resort urge a conference.'[19] Two days later, on the 29 August, Malcolm Christie reported to London the views of his principal contact, codenamed 'Knight', who claimed that 'Hitler's stock stands lower today amongst the German people than at any time since prior to the march into the Rhineland.' 'Knight', Christie reported, thought Hitler was hesitating and bluffing and urged London to make no concessions: 'We have his whole position undermined, keep it so.' A second contact in Switzerland, Isaak Jammerbein, told Christie that there was serious evidence of unrest in Germany – food riots in the cities and ugly scenes at stations where reservists were being called to the colours – and urged again a policy of firmness.[20] On 30 August Goerdeler himself sent a telegram to the British Foreign Office, insisting that 'Chief manager's [Hitler's] attitude weakening. Remain completely firm. No compromise.'[21] All these reports were so much wishful thinking.

The British gave more serious attention to the signals that there might be divisions to exploit in the National Socialist leadership. For some time there had been a belief that Field Marshal Hermann Göring, head of the German air force, plenipotentiary for Germany's economic Four-Year Plan, and widely regarded as second only to Hitler, might stage some kind of political coup or could be used to engineer Hitler to accept a peaceful solution. During

August 1939 an unusual avenue opened up which allowed the British leadership to exploit this possibility. Early in the month a Swedish businessman, Birger Dahlerus, organized a meeting between a number of British contacts and Göring, at a house in Schleswig-Holstein, near the Danish border. In his memoir of his amateur diplomacy Dahlerus confessed that he had long harboured a desire to bring the British and German people together to avoid any possibility of a second great war and thought that Göring, whom he had known for some years, and who seemed to share this desire, would be the best person to involve from the German side. When Dahlerus met Halifax on 25 July to explain his plan, the British foreign secretary refused to involve the government, but wished the project well. The meeting went ahead on 6–8 August, and Dahlerus was sufficiently encouraged by Göring's sympathetic reaction to the idea of a conference to try to find a way to get official British endorsement. Dahlerus later wrote that he spent day and night trying to get the British to discuss a conference: 'It was inexplicable to me,' he wrote, 'that with the issues at stake, there was not a determined person to force a cabinet meeting . . . and all this time the Field-Marshal was waiting to be informed whether the English were interested.' The situation changed only after the German–Soviet pact. Lord Halifax finally agreed to meet Dahlerus on the evening of 25 August; he thanked him for his efforts but then told him that since official negotiations were now in place, Dahlerus' 'assistance would no longer be necessary'.[22]

Dahlerus nevertheless persisted, and the following day

he persuaded Halifax to write a personal letter to Göring emphasizing the British desire for peace. Dahlerus then flew to Berlin and delivered the letter, and in the early hours of 27 August he was invited to meet Hitler for the first time. During the conversation that followed Dahlerus recalled Hitler's complaint that 'like some unsuccessful suitor, he had repeatedly endeavoured to urge Downing Street to collaborate, but in vain.'[23] Hitler implored Dahlerus to return to London to encourage the British to accept his offer of an agreement and a guarantee for the Empire, and the following day Dahlerus met both Chamberlain and Halifax, who gave him a private note to take back to Berlin of the minimum the British could accept. The note contained substantially the same points as the letter at that moment being drafted for Henderson to take back to Hitler. Dahlerus was smuggled to Heston airport and flew back to Berlin, his shuttle diplomacy now, so he believed, at the centre of world history.

It is difficult to decide exactly what the two sides expected to achieve from the Dahlerus discussions. He was an unconventional emissary, and his intervention almost certainly made things worse, as it persuaded Chamberlain and Halifax that the opening to Göring represented a real division in German high politics, while at the same time it convinced Hitler that if the British were so desperate as to communicate unofficially, their willingness in the end to support Poland must be called into question. The British side found Dahlerus hard to take altogether seriously. He was immediately nicknamed 'the Walrus' by the Foreign Office. Richard Butler thought him an 'honest little man', but out of his depth in a world where international affairs could not be treated as if they were 'items of dispute in some business deal'.[24] The British leadership did not tell the French about the talks, and concealed their discussions as much as possible. Dahlerus was useful only as a barometer of German attitudes. The Foreign Office later dismissed him as an 'arch-appeaser'.[25] On the German side the motives are more complex. Göring was not on the point of staging a coup against his leader, but he was almost certainly anxious to avoid a general war and every bit as sympathetic to the idea of a possible agreement with Britain as Hitler. It is likely too that Göring was put out by Ribbentrop's success over the German–Soviet pact and hoped that he could cap it by securing a British agreement. His connection with Dahlerus explains Hitler's decision to encourage Göring after 25 August to put additional pressure on the British to increase their hesitancy over war. Dahlerus mattered to Hitler only to the extent that he was another iron in the fire in his brief attempt to dislocate the alliance against him.[26] The ploy did succeed in creating a distraction at a critical diplomatic juncture. As late as 31 August, on the eve of the German attack on Poland, the announcement that a Reich Defence Council had been established with Göring as chair prompted the sudden hope at the British embassy in Berlin that at the last moment a coup to oust Hitler had actually taken place.[27]

Dahlerus was in reality superfluous to the greater

game played out in the final days of peace. Hitler did not regard the initiatives from the Western side as anything other than further evidence that the threat of a general European war could be averted. Almost as soon as the first order to march had been cancelled, he ordered preparations for a second planned invasion. Halder on 27 August told the army Quartermaster-General that the earliest date on which mobilization could be completed again was Thursday 31 August, though he hoped that by then the British would have been negotiated into agreement.[28] On 28 August Hitler confirmed that the attack would begin on the morning of 1 September, while German troops moved from their resting stations once again. Bernd Engelmann, a young soldier who had flirted with the socialist resistance earlier in the 1930s, found himself woken late at night by the mobilization siren and the order to move out from barracks. His companion gloated, 'Now the Polack's goose is cooked! Next week we'll be in Warsaw, and then it'll be on to the east.' The unit was posted instead to a small hotel on the banks of the Rhine, where it waited for orders. Everything was done with complete radio silence, and since Engelmann was part of a signals unit there was nothing to do except to make occasional trips into the nearby city where his relatives lived, all certain this time that 'war was imminent'.[29]

After the sudden decision to cancel on the previous Friday, Hitler took every opportunity to announce that Britain and France would not ultimately fight, even if they took the crisis to the very end, a view that Ribbentrop repeatedly parroted. One of Hitler's military adjutants noted in his diary that Hitler only wanted to solve the Polish question: 'With the others he wanted no war at all.'[30] Goebbels found Hitler 'very confident'; the watchword was 'to take up an attitude and keep one's nerve'.[31] Over the remaining four days of peace Hitler continued to pursue the goal not only of isolating Poland, but also of ensuring that the Poles would be seen to be in the wrong by rejecting German proposals. The object once again was to create circumstances which might make it more difficult for Britain and France to honour their pledges. A more skilful diplomat might well have made capital from such a strategy, but everything Hitler did during the brief period in which he tried to operate it made the situation worse rather than better. The starting point for the last diplomatic game was the letter which Hitler was waiting for Henderson to deliver from London in response to his offer of 25 August. The letter when it was finally delivered by the British ambassador on the evening of 28 August put Poland firmly in the middle once again.

In the desperate diplomacy of the days since the German–Soviet pact, Poland had featured less and less in the calculation of the Western states. The note to Hitler reasserted Poland's significance and made it clear once again that German–Polish relations remained the key to war or peace. On 28 August Halifax got the British ambassador in Warsaw, Sir Hugh Kennard, to ask Beck if the British could tell Berlin that the Polish side was prepared for conversations. This decision has to be understood not as the first tentative steps towards a new Munich, but as a sign that the British government believed Hitler's willingness to talk might be a measure of his willingness to climb down from war (a view which could scarcely be supported by anything in Hitler's earlier record except Munich). The Polish government nevertheless took heart that the indication on the part of the German government that they were prepared to discuss the issues might signal a changed atmosphere, and Beck agreed to the British request. On 29 August Beck assembled a group of Foreign Office officials in his house in Warsaw to choose a Polish plenipotentiary for talks with Germany and to decide where the meeting should take place. It was agreed that the Polish negotiators would not go to Berlin under any circumstances. Instead the officials recommended meeting in a small town near the Polish–German border, perhaps in a railway carriage in order to prevent any attempt by the German side to overawe the Polish delegates. The role of principal Polish negotiator finally fell to the Polish ambassador to Germany, Józef Lipski.[32] The Polish government then waited to see the outcome of the discussion scheduled to take place between Hitler and Henderson that evening. In the meantime the decision to order general mobilization was postponed in case this affected the chance for negotiation. Not until 3 o'clock in the afternoon of 30 August, when it was evident that discussions would probably break down, was the order given. Mobilization was announced to the Polish public two hours later. Valuable time to prepare for the German assault had been lost by the Polish army.[33]

For the final three days of the crisis leading to war the spotlight fell on a man quite unaccustomed to its glare. Nevile Henderson has been regarded as a generally malign influence in the last months of peace, an appeaser committed at all costs to avoiding war with Germany and a reluctant emissary. 'The responsibility of my small job in Berlin,' he wrote to Horace Wilson in May 1939, 'is greater than my capacity and I cannot feel otherwise than profoundly pessimistic.'[34] Henderson never made any secret of the fact that he thought the Polish guarantee was mistaken, since it reduced Britain's room for manoeuvre entirely. He was also less confident than the government in London that there was any real chance of avoiding conflict: 'my belief,' he wrote to Halifax earlier in August, 'is that, if driven into a corner, Hitler will choose war.'[35] But Henderson was as unwilling to grant Hitler a free hand against Poland as his political masters in London, and his three days of negotiation in late August over the possibility of a truce and conference between Germany and Poland showed that even appeasers had clear limits. On 28 August Henderson arrived at the Reich chancellery by car from the British embassy. He was unable to go until 10.30 in the evening because of the need to translate the British reply. He was wearing a dark red carnation buttonhole, which he had done every day of his embassy in Berlin, except for the three days preceding the Munich crisis, when, as he told German journalists, it seemed 'inappropriate'. Hitler's chancellery chief, Otto Meissner, welcomed Henderson and observed with evident relief the presence of the flower.[36] Hitler that evening was 'calm, even conciliatory', Henderson thought. Hitler took the letter and after an hour in which Henderson tried to persuade him of the good sense in compromising with Poland, promised an answer the following day.

Throughout 29 August there was a growing hope that a real possibility had been created for genuine negotiation. 'We are at the culminating point of the crisis,' wrote a French Foreign Office official in his diary.[37] While in Warsaw preparations were made for the start of negotiations, British leaders considered that the latest secret intelligence from Berlin made it evident that Hitler was hesitating, faced with the prospect of internal dissent and Western firmness. Dahlerus telephoned Halifax from Berlin to say that 'he thought things were satisfactory', and in the German Foreign Office the anti-war Ernst von Weizsäcker sensed 'a greater optimism'.[38] But when Henderson returned to the chancellery that evening to meet Hitler at 7.15 the atmosphere was quite different from the night before. Hitler handed him the German reply and he and Ribbentrop stood and watched as Henderson read it. The demands it contained were an unacceptable basis for any discussion: the return of Danzig and the entire Corridor territory, safeguards for the other German minorities living in Poland, and the necessity of involving the Soviet Union in any settlement in Poland. At the end of the reply Henderson read the demand that the Polish government send a negotiator with full powers to sign by the following day, 30 August. Henderson angrily replied that this final request 'had the sound of an ultimatum'. Hitler denied it, and the rest of the interview, Henderson later recalled, had a 'somewhat stormy character'. As he left the building, Henderson remarked to Meissner that he was afraid he would probably never wear a carnation in Germany again.[39]

The following day the crisis reached a climax. Henderson telephoned the results of his argument with Hitler to London. 'It looked pretty bad,' Halifax later commented; he immediately began work on a draft of a sharply worded reply. Henderson received a preliminary response by 4 a.m., which explained that it was unreasonable to request a Polish plenipotentiary at 24 hours' notice. Further letters followed during the day inviting the German government to suspend the war of nerves and violence directed at Poland and to extend a formal invitation to the Polish ambassador for his government to consider a set of definite written proposals. No pressure was put on the Polish government to comply, and Warsaw did nothing, since no formal request had been made from the German side asking for a negotiator. The situation was confused by yet another intervention from Göring, who sent Dahlerus to London with a modified offer of a plebiscite in the Corridor instead of outright annexation. This, too, could be seen as evidence of German uncertainty. Halifax made it clear that no demands could be met if they amounted to 'dictation on the Czecho-Slovak model'.[40] Dahlerus was asked to telephone Göring directly to see if a meeting place outside Germany would be acceptable. Since a city in Italy was a likely suggestion, the war minister asked Halifax to ensure that a conference, if it did take place, would not be on Axis territory.[41] Göring rejected the idea out of hand, insisting once again that a Polish emissary must arrive within 24 hours and must come to Berlin 'where the Chancellor was'. Dahlerus flew back to Germany for the last time. 'I can't help thinking,' wrote Alexander Cadogan, Halifax's under-secretary, in his diary, 'Germans are in an awful fix.'[42]

By the end of the day the situation was at deadlock. Henderson asked to see Ribbentrop and was invited to the German Foreign Office at 11.30. He postponed his arrival until he had time to have the latest letter from London deciphered; this once again reiterated the need for restraint on both sides and called for assurances from the Germans that they would end any threat of violence. Henderson met Ribbentrop at midnight in what has since become a notorious confrontation. While Henderson read out the British suggestions Ribbentrop kept leaping to his feet arguing angrily, crossing his arms, asking Henderson whether he had finished or not. The ambassador's patience was exhausted and the two men grew more heated. Paul Schmidt, the chief interpreter, later wrote that Henderson gradually lost his 'calm, typically English reserve'. His face grew crimson and his hands shook.[43] When Henderson remarked that his government had news that Germans were committing acts of sabotage in Poland, Ribbentrop leapt to his feet: 'That's a shameful lie of the Polish government,' he shouted. 'I can tell you, Herr Henderson, that the situation is damned serious!'

Henderson waved his finger at Ribbentrop and shouted, 'You have even said "damned"! That is not the language of a statesman in so serious a situation.' The two men glared at each other, breathing heavily. Schmidt later wrote that he had never seen anything like it before, and wondered what his job was supposed to be when words were abandoned in favour of blows, which he expected at any moment.[44]

After a few minutes, both men recovered their self-control. Ribbentrop then produced his own document, a list of sixteen articles representing the German demands to Poland. He read them, Henderson recalled, at great speed in an angry and scornful voice so that it was impossible for the ambassador to understand clearly what the proposals amounted to. Ribbentrop in the memoirs he wrote in prison at Nuremberg in 1946 denied that he had spoken either angrily or at speed; Schmidt recalled that Ribbentrop read them in a normal way, adding further explanation as he went along. [45] Henderson was almost certainly too flustered by the argument to listen fully to what Ribbentrop was saying. When Ribbentrop had finished, Henderson asked for the text of the document so the contents could be conveyed to London and Warsaw, but Ribbentrop contemptuously refused. He threw the paper on the desk in front of him and announced that since no Polish plenipotentiary had arrived within the stated deadline, the German proposals were now redundant. Henderson left the confrontation, he later wrote, 'convinced that the last hope for peace had vanished'.[46] The gist of the 'sixteen points' was finally conveyed the following morning by Dahlerus, at Goring's instigation, but the full text was not formally handed over until 9.15 in the evening of 31 August, by which time the attack on Poland was about to begin. The Polish ambassador to Berlin tried to see either Hitler or Ribbentrop in order to ascertain what possibility remained for discussions, but was refused. He was finally able to see Ribbentrop for a few minutes, earlier that evening at 6 o'clock, but when he said he had no power to agree to anything, he was dismissed. Telephone communication between Berlin and Warsaw was severed.[47]

During the days in which the prospects for a genuine negotiation were fruitlessly explored, the outlook among those beyond the inner circle of negotiators and among the wider public also grew more optimistic. Little of what was actually argued over at the diplomatic level, either officially or unofficially, could be made public, and rumour about German hesitation fuelled both optimism and uncertainty. Henry 'Chips' Channon reflected the mood in his diary entry on 30 August: 'All day we were on a see-saw Peace-War-Peace.'[48] General Ironside told the MP Edward Spears that Chamberlain himself now thought 'there would be no war'; Lord Chatfield, British minister for the co-ordination of defence, looking 'very cheerful', told another MP that Hitler was showing 'distinct signs of weakening'.[49] Harold Nicolson was told that the Polish ambassador to London thought 'things are going very nicely', and the general mood of the House of Commons was, Nicolson thought, 'more cheerful' than it had been for days.[50] The wider public also displayed a growing optimism. A diary written by a schoolgirl for the Mass Observation survey a few days later recorded the following scene after she had arrived at school: 'The general feeling was optimistic. There was a murmur of assent all round when the history mistress affirmed that "this evacuation business was a brilliant propaganda stroke of Mr Chamberlain. He only did it to fool Hitler into submission. No possibility of war now."'[51]

The mood in France also swung unsteadily between expectation of war and hope of agreement. Political circles in France were even more remote from the final round of diplomacy, and rumour flourished. There was optimism that Italian leaders had now given clear indications that Italy would remain neutral in any coming conflict, ending the danger of a two-front war, although even this news was far from certain. The French Foreign Office was nevertheless increasingly pessimistic by 30 August, and rumours circulated about a sudden German air attack on London, Paris and Warsaw. The prevailing view was that at all costs the line must be held against Hitler's threat. 'We have had enough of it,' wrote André Maurois in an article in *Le Figaro*. 'We do not want violence, hatred and lies to be considered the highest virtues. We have had enough of it.'[52] On 31 August, however, the rumour spread that acceptable terms had been agreed between Poland and Germany. Maurois and his friends 'thought the game had been won' and returned home, 'mad with joy'.[53] The efforts of Bonnet to use the prospect of negotiations between Poland and Germany as a further bridge to a peaceful solution were nonetheless rejected by most French politicians as preparation for a second Munich. On the evening of 31 August Daladier summoned a cabinet meeting to thrash out the French position. During the discussion he deliberately turned his back on Bonnet to indicate the gap that now existed between the hardliners and the *munichois*. At a critical moment in the arguments Daladier chose to read out a letter from Robert Coulondre, the French ambassador in Berlin, which he had actually received six days before. 'The trial of strength turns to our advantage,' Daladier read out in a loud voice. 'It is only necessary to hold, hold, hold.' The letter proved a turning-point in the discussion and ended Bonnet's hopes for compromise. In France the view still flourished that Hitler really was bluffing and would be deterred by a show of firmness.[54]

The ambivalence about the real possibility of war in both states was in marked contrast to the situation in Berlin. Hitler's purpose in encouraging further talks, both formal and informal, was to create exactly this sense of uncertainty, but he was now more certain than before about waging war. The apparent willingness to accept negotiation was a ploy, designed to show that Germany had right on its side when no Polish negotiator appeared. Even the role of Göring, whatever his private fears about Western intervention, was manipulated to create maximum confusion. When pressed, Göring, just like Hitler, regarded the return of Danzig, the settlement of the Corridor and the summoning of a Polish representative at short notice as a minimum condition. The final scene between Henderson and Ribbentrop made it evident that no real negotiation had ever been envisaged on the German side. Instead the interval between the cancellation and the final invasion of Poland on 1 September was used to bombard the German public with inflammatory propaganda against the Poles. Details of Polish 'atrocities' were magnified by the German press; publicity was given to alleged reports that Germans living in Poland had been castrated. All of this was designed to ensure that the outside world would understand the German *casus belli*, and that the German public would wage a Polish war with sufficient enthusiasm after years in which they had become accustomed to the bloodless victories achieved by threats, menaces and bluff.

During the last days of peace Hitler also ordered preparations for the start of what was to be a 'race war' in the east. The head of the police and SS, Heinrich Himmler, was charged with creating special action groups (*Einsatzgruppen*) that would follow the soldiers into Poland to round up Poland's political, cultural and intellectual elite and murder them. Planning was started in July and a directive drawn up in August.[55] By the end of August five groups had been created, each assigned to a German army, to carry out 'Operation Tannenberg'. Two further groups were formed shortly after the start of hostilities. In addition, 20,000 members of the regular police force were assigned to security duties in Poland to help with the 'pacification' process. In the first days of the invasion these security forces murdered ethnic Poles and Polish Jews, burnt down synagogues and arrested or shot Polish soldiers who had lost contact with their retreating forces. The destruction of the Polish elite was to pave the way for the Germanization of the conquered areas.[56] The conflict that Hitler envisaged, which would destroy the Polish state, had an agenda drawn not from diplomacy or military strategy, but from the racial priorities of the regime in establishing German 'living space' and uniting all ethnic Germans in the east with the new Reich.[57]

Earlier the same day, 30 August, Hitler met with Keitel and Brauchitsch to authorize preparations for an attack to begin at 4.45 on the morning of 1 September. He also met with Albert Forster, the National Socialist leader in Danzig, and discussed arrangements for the seizure of the city two days later.[58] Hitler was determined not to abandon war a second time. Some of the senior party leaders had doubts that the war would be localized. Göring complained to Goebbels that they had not built Germany up in six years 'in order to risk it all in war'.[59] Goebbels observed in his diary that the risk seemed much greater than Hitler realized, but he was told again, 'Führer does not believe England will intervene.'[60] At midday on 31 August Hitler published 'Directive No. 1 for the Conduct of the War' and at 4 p.m. gave the armed forces the order to attack. He told Halder that 'France and England will not march' and assured Brauchitsch that the war would be 'localized', a view that the general insisted on when he was pressed by Weizsäcker to do something to prevent a catastrophe. 'Don't you read the newspapers?' Weizsäcker asked, to which Brauchitsch replied with a shrug of the shoulders.[61] General Wilhelm Ritter von Leeb, preparing a possible defence on the German frontier in the west, was also told that Brauchitsch thought war in the west would not happen and hoped for localization. Even on 2 September Brauchitsch telephoned von Leeb with the news that the British and French ambassadors had not after all been withdrawn and that in his view 'bridges were not completely broken' in the war of nerves Hitler was playing with the West.[62]

German forces rolled into position during the evening of 31 August. To give a spurious justification for war, a special operation was mounted by Himmler's deputy and head of the Security Police, Reinhard Heydrich. Early in August he had called a number of senior SS officers to a meeting in the ballroom of the Hotel Oberschlesien in the small German town of Gleiwitz, near the Polish border. He told them that a way had to be found to show that Poland was the aggressor when war broke out. The plan, approved by Hitler, was to stage a mock Polish attack on Hochlinden customs post, the Pitschen forestry lodge and the radio transmitter station at Gleiwitz. Heydrich appointed a Security Service (SD) officer, Alfred Naujocks, to lead the raid. Polish uniforms were requested from Admiral Canaris, head of counter-intelligence, and six prisoners from Sachsenhausen concentration camp were chosen to be dressed as Polish soldiers and shot. During the afternoon of 31 August, Heydrich telephoned with the codewords 'Grandmother dead!' to signal the start of the operation. In the evening the German security officers occupied the Gleiwitz radio station and faked a brief Polish broadcast. German troops pretended to return fire. The bodies of the six prisoners were left lying at the Hochlinden customs post. Another corpse was supplied by the Gestapo, a pro-Polish German from Silesia, Franz Honiok, arrested on the previous day. His bullet-riddled body was dropped at the doorway to the radio station, the first act of barbarism in a barbarous war.[63]

Local War or World War?

1–3 September

At 4.45 in the morning the German training ship *Schleswig Holstein*, moored off the port of Danzig, opened fire on the Polish fort at Westerplatte, launching the Second World War. The ship had been sent from Germany on 23 August and arrived at Danzig two days later allegedly on a goodwill visit, but in reality to be in place for the start of war on 26 August. The ship had been forced to stay in place for six more days until the codeword 'Fishing' was finally sent out and the seizure of Danzig could begin. Fifteen minutes after the firing began, the National Socialist Albert Forster, who had been unconstitutionally declared the chief authority in Danzig on 24 August, announced on the radio the reunification of the city with the German Reich. The church bells began to peal and over the city hall a large swastika banner was unfurled. Gestapo officers, reinforced by SS and SA men, seized Polish officials, teachers and priests, using lists prepared in advance, and marched them to the Victoria School, which was set up as a temporary camp. Opponents of the party were driven through the streets and beaten or in some cases murdered. Raids were made on the houses of Jews still living in Danzig. The following day work was accelerated on a concentration camp nearby at Stutthof to house the new wave of prisoners.[1]

The military situation in Danzig developed rapidly in the first few hours. The railway bridge over the river Weichsel was seized. Most Polish security points were captured except for the main post office and the Westerplatte fort, where Polish soldiers guarded a large munitions store. The post office was secured that day, but the Westerplatte held out until 7 September after a bitter contest. Throughout western Poland German air force units bombed Polish positions and military strongpoints and attacked factories and bases far in the rear of Polish armies. Three German army groups moved forward, one against the Polish Corridor, one towards Upper Silesia and the third from East Prussia. They faced stiff resistance in places, but Polish armies were pushed back under relentless pressure; some of the small Polish air force had been destroyed at its bases. Polish civilians were told about the German attack during the morning, but many of them could already see the result of air bombardment all around them. 'Everybody is talking about war,' wrote Zygmunt Klukowski in his diary, 'and everybody is sure that we will win.' He found himself surrounded by waves of refugees moving away from the threatened western zones of the country. Rumours sprang up that the Polish army had managed to seize Danzig. Attempts to prepare a blackout against expected air attacks were hampered by the sudden disappearance from the shops of nails, black material and tape.[2]

The day the war started was Hitler's day. He had taken the final irrevocable decision and was now at last Germany's war leader. At 10 in the morning he arrived at the Kroll Opera House in Berlin to address the German parliament. He wore a field-grey jacket ordered by his valet a few days before, instead of the usual brown party uniform. Because the session was only summoned at 3 a.m., over a hundred deputies from outlying areas had been unable to arrive in time or were already in the armed forces, and their places were allegedly taken by men of Hitler's bodyguard and other party officials. The Reichstag president, Hermann Göring, announced that the proxy deputies could also vote, to avoid giving the impression of anything other than unanimity.[3] Hitler received a storm of applause from the assembled company. He gave a shorter speech than usual, blaming the Poles for their intransigence and their final act of aggression and elaborating all his efforts for a peaceful solution. 'Danzig was and is a German city,' he announced. 'The Corridor was and is German.' Without German culture, he claimed, the whole region would have been plunged in 'the deepest barbarism'.[4] He said nothing particularly hostile about Britain and France. During the speech he was seen to glance often at the diplomatic box, where British and French representatives also sat. When he had finished, there was a standing ovation. 'Strong decisiveness,' observed Goebbels in his diary. Hitler had also announced that if he was to die or be killed in the conflict his place would be taken by Hermann Göring; if Göring perished too, the new leader was to be his party deputy, Rudolf Hess.[5] The interior minister, Wilhelm Frick, then read out the new law uniting Danzig with the Reich, which was approved by unanimous acclamation. Hitler returned to the chancellery, 'bathed in sweat and exhausted', through the large crowds that had gathered to see him on Unter den Linden and the Wilhelmstrasse.[6] During the day a number of decrees and orders came into force for the war effort. The most significant was Hitler's approval of the 'euthanasia' killing of the physically and mentally disabled, which bore the date 1 September when it was found among German records after the war. The order had been held in abeyance during the summer, and was in fact not finally authorized until October. It was designed both to free medical resources and facilities for the war effort and to rid the nation of what was defined as a genetic burden. As a result of the instructions over 70,000 disabled or chronically sick Germans were murdered.[7] It was backdated in order to emphasize the close link in Hitler's mind between the onset of the German war effort and the need to cleanse the race of any internal threat.

The news of the German action in Poland arrived early in the morning in London and Paris. At 7 a.m. Cadogan was alerted to the incorporation of Danzig into the Reich and a little later was told about the invasion. A Reuters telegram arrived for the prime minister at 7.48 detailing a Berlin wireless announcement made earlier that morning about Hitler's decision for war with Poland: 'Order put an end to this lunacy,' ran the translation, 'eye [*sic*] have no other choice than meet force with force from now on.'⁸ The British war minister, Hore-Belisha, was telephoned at home by General Gort at 7.20 to be told 'Germans were over'. He rolled over in bed muttering, 'damned Germans, to be awakened in this way'. When he got up he found his barber had not appeared and realized he would have to shave himself.⁹ It was not yet entirely clear what had happened or how reliable the news was. Very late the previous evening a German wireless report had been brought to Chamberlain announcing that *Polish* troops had crossed the German frontier in three or four places.¹⁰ When Halifax called the German chargé d'affaires for clarification he was told that the embassy would make enquiries; the Polish ambassador however confirmed that war had indeed broken out, and that Germany was the aggressor. In Paris news arrived from the French ambassador in Warsaw at 8.30 that the German army was attacking all along the frontier.¹¹ Shortly afterwards both Chamberlain and Daladier gave the order for general mobilization and evacuation of children and mothers from the main cities, while the two governments prepared to co-ordinate the delivery in Berlin of a note demanding the immediate withdrawal of German forces from Polish soil. In Washington, hours behind European time, Roosevelt was told the news by telephone at 2.50 in the morning from the American embassy in Paris, which had been alerted to the invasion by the ambassador in Warsaw. Within a few minutes Roosevelt, had ordered that all United States naval vessels and all United States army commands should be warned by radio immediately.[12]

The instructions sent out to the British services for general mobilization reflected a curious ambivalence. The cabinet military secretary, Hastings Ismay, informed the chiefs of staff that the cabinet had decided to send a telegram to Berlin which was not an ultimatum but amounted to an ultimatum. 'It is possible,' he added laconically, 'that you will wish to give your commanders both at home and overseas some intimation that this virtual ultimatum has been despatched.'[13] The chief of the air staff, Cyril Newall, duly sent a telegram to all commanders in Britain, the Mediterranean, Palestine, Iraq, Aden and the Far East to say that 'virtually an ultimatum' was about to be delivered and to prepare for sudden German attacks.[14]

During the day the messages to Berlin were carefully drafted. The British note asked for assurances that aggression against Poland had been stopped and that 'German troops have been withdrawn'. This last phrase was then altered to 'will be promptly withdrawn' to make it easier for the Germans to comply quickly. If no assurances were received, the note concluded, the British government would 'without hesitation fulfil their obligation to Poland'.[15] Parliament was then summoned to meet at 6 in the evening so that Chamberlain could announce the 'virtual ultimatum'.

By the time MPs arrived, the House was already darkened to conform with the blackout regulations imposed by mobilization; sandbags and anti-gas doors installed during the previous week gave the impression that war had already broken out. Chamberlain entered to a loud cheer, and began to speak of the grave responsibility that now lay in his hands to accept 'the awful arbitrament of war'. When he placed the blame for the crisis squarely on the shoulders of Hitler and his 'senseless ambition' he gave a rare sign of emotion, raising his voice and striking the despatch box with a clenched fist, eliciting a further cheer. After he announced that Hitler's sixteen points had not even been communicated to the Poles (which was not quite the truth), the Conservative MP Nancy Astor called out, 'Well I never did!'[16] He finally read out the document that was to be given to Hitler; as he finished, another member called out 'Time limit?' Chamberlain said he did not expect a favourable reply, in which case the ambassador would ask for his passports (the equivalent of a state of war); but he failed to specify how long he would wait for Hitler's response.[17]

Meanwhile, in Paris the atmosphere was still affected by the optimism of the previous few days. Some officials and politicians thought that Hitler would continue to prevaricate, others that Poland and Germany would reach a face-saving agreement. 'In all cases,' noted Boyer de Sainte-Suzanne, 'many do not believe in a war.'[18] A message was prepared based on the British text, and despite the opposition of Bonnet and others it was despatched to the French ambassador in Berlin. At 9.30 in the evening Beck asked the French ambassador in Warsaw why nothing had yet been done to honour the pledge to come to Poland's assistance, but at exactly that moment in Berlin Nevile Henderson had arrived to communicate the British note to Ribbentrop at the German Foreign Office. Half an hour later, the French ambassador followed suit. Henderson asked for an immediate answer.[19]

The response in Berlin was a puzzled one. Hitler's valet heard him say after news of the British and French notes arrived, 'We will now see if they come to Poland's aid. They'll chicken out again.'[20] Party functionaries gathered in the chancellery lobbies still thought the West was bluffing. Hitler was unable to decide if the notes were formal ultimatums or not. Henderson had been told by the Foreign Office, according to Halifax's later recollection, that he was authorized to say that the note '*was* a warning and not an ultimatum', though he did not relay this to Ribbentrop.[21] Among the German public there was similar uncertainty about what the result would be of real war. Shirer noticed unusually crowded cafés and bars in Berlin. The German government, unlike the British and French, had not yet ordered evacuation of sections of the population, but at 8.15 in the evening there was a sudden air-raid siren and the streets emptied as people rushed for the cellars and shelters. It was a false alarm, but it created, Shirer thought, a widespread apprehension exacerbated by the experience of the blackout.[22] The German–Jewish linguist Victor Klemperer, living in Dresden, found a confused response among his acquaintances to the news of war with Poland. One boy told him that Britain and France would remain neutral; another that 'The English are cowards, they won't do anything!'; a shop-girl announced that in her view English neutrality was a joke. In his diary he wrote: 'still no declaration of war on their side. Is it coming or will they fail to resist and merely demonstrate weakness?'[23]

In Britain and France there was a sense of unreal expectation, 'greyout rather than blackout', as the journalist Malcolm Muggeridge put it.[24] The blackout that descended all over Britain on the evening of 1 September was nevertheless real enough and made war seem more apparent: 'on the very verge of war,' wrote Sir Henry Channon, after watching his servants frantically hanging blackout curtains.[25] 'Nothing could be more dramatic or give one more of a shock,' wrote Harold Nicolson, than to find a perfectly black city, 'a pall of black velvet'.[26] Among MPs there was also a sense of puzzlement about the failure to give a time limit for the withdrawal of German troops when it was evident that Britain and France would have to honour their commitment to Poland. Rumours began to circulate that the Italians had made an offer to mediate and that the French were hoping to seize the opportunity to abandon the Poles. Harold Macmillan, the future prime minister and a Conservative critic of Chamberlain, later described a mood of 'confusion' and 'suspicion' surrounding the failure to make a clear statement of Britain's intention to declare war, and historians have shared in the view that the delay could only be explained by the continued search for an appeasing way out of the sudden crisis.[27]

A number of factors contributed to the delay in making a final declaration of war. The first difficulty was the request from the French military leadership that the outbreak of war should be postponed if possible for two or three days while they completed the evacuation of Paris and the frontier areas. The priority was to ensure that the *couverture* – the main defence of the frontier – was in place before German air attacks began to disrupt it. French commanders contrasted the low level of British mobilization with the requirement to move some six million French reservists into position. The expectation was that German air forces would do in France what they were doing in Poland, although it should have been evident at the time that the German air force simply lacked the capacity to do so.[28] Since there was no intention of giving immediate military assistance to Poland, the argument for carrying out an orderly mobilization and deployment did not seem at the time unreasonable. The delay caused by mobilization nevertheless made it difficult for the British and French governments to co-ordinate their declarations of war, which was regarded as desirable, particularly on the British side where there were suspicions harboured about French good faith. The arguments between the two sides over the mobilization arrangements continued into the very last hours of 2 September, when Bonnet still hoped to be able to delay the French declaration for a further two days.

The second and more controversial explanation was the sudden intervention of Mussolini in a crisis in which he was otherwise a marginal figure. The idea of a conference brokered by Italy had been around for almost a week, from the time that Ciano telephoned Halifax to suggest that he and Mussolini stood ready to work for a 'peaceful solution'.[29] Over the next few days Mussolini began to regret his decision to abandon the commitment to Germany, and a number of preliminary mobilization measures were put into operation, including a blackout. These precautions were prompted partly by a fear that Britain and France might act against Italy regardless of the fact that the decision not to intervene had already been taken. On 31 August Ciano suggested to Mussolini the idea of a major European conference to be called on 5 September to thrash out all the remaining problems generated by the Treaty of Versailles. The proposal was forwarded to Halifax and Bonnet.[30] There were strong echoes of the Czech crisis the year before, when Mussolini's intervention, at Western prompting, appeared to bring Hitler to the conference table, and it may well be that Mussolini hoped to seize back a major role by achieving a similar outcome. It is also tempting to argue that the conference proposal was a piece of deliberate mischief-making, to confuse the British and French and allow Germany to achieve a coup in Poland while discussions continued. Ciano himself may well have supported the proposal in order to prevent Mussolini from reverting to the idea once again of possible belligerency. At a cabinet meeting on 1 September, after news of the German invasion, Mussolini was clearly anxious about the Italian failure to join the war and the possibility that he might appear a 'traitor' in German eyes. He had already taken the precaution of asking Hitler to say publicly that he released Italy from its obligation, but the whiff of treachery made Mussolini ill-at-ease and ill-tempered with his cabinet colleagues when some chose to discuss it.[31]

Whatever Mussolini's motives, the driving force behind acceptance of the conference proposal was Bonnet and his allies in the French government who still wanted to withdraw from the prospect of war if it were possible to do so. On the evening of 31 August Bonnet hoped to be able to respond favourably to Ciano's suggestion but could get no positive response from London, where the idea had already been rejected after finding Daladier 'pretty unfavourable'.[32] Daladier argued with Bonnet over the conference but then allowed him to continue exploring its possibility, struck by a sudden moment of characteristic irresolution. The following day Bonnet made strenuous efforts to get the suggestion of a conference publicly known and, if possible, endorsed by Britain. He also let the German Foreign Office know that France accepted the suggestion of a conference. To make it appear to be the official French position, which it was not, he sent a press communiqué to the Havas news agency that night: 'The French government has discussed an Italian initiative to bring about a peaceful settlement of Europe's problems, and has signified an agreement.'[33] To delay any British attempt to send a premature ultimatum, Bonnet insisted to Halifax that no declaration of war, and hence no ultimatum, could be made or sent until the French Chamber of Deputies had met on 2 September. Not until the afternoon of that day was a phone call received from Paris which explained it was not the case that only parliament could declare war and that once war credits were voted, Daladier could ask the French president to announce a state of war.[34] Nor was it made sufficiently clear to the British side that Daladier had no intention of putting the issue to a parliamentary vote, perhaps uncertain of the extent to which it would provoke divisions in the chamber.

On the morning of 2 September Bonnet continued to pressure the Italian Foreign Office to communicate the idea of a conference to Hitler. Ciano rang Bonnet in the early afternoon after he had heard Hitler's response. Hitler wanted to know if the two notes of the previous evening were ultimatums or not, and secondly if he could postpone an answer to the idea of a conference until midday on 3 September. Hitler almost certainly regarded the proposal as an opportunity to further confuse the Western states, whose firmness he had always doubted, while the extra day would see German forces deep inside Polish territory and the Corridor captured. Goebbels noted in his diary that Hitler also thought he might gain something if he held on to the conquered territory in Poland while attending a conference, but later in the morning he told Goebbels that the British and French would have to abandon their virtual ultimatums of the night before if anything was going to come of a meeting.[35] Bonnet replied in the affirmative to both of Hitler's questions, without consulting his government, though he did tell Ciano that he would have to see what Chamberlain and Daladier both thought of the proposal. For Chamberlain the intervention must have seemed at least worth exploring. A few weeks before, in July, he had told

Daladier that in his view 'Mussolini is the one man who can influence Hitler to keep the peace.'[36]

Ciano next telephoned Halifax from Rome to explain that Hitler had not immediately rejected the idea but needed a day's postponement before giving an answer. Halifax said he would inform Chamberlain about the proposal, but the condition for any discussion was not simply an armistice, as Ciano suggested, but 'the withdrawal of German troops from Polish soil'.[37] Halifax then rushed to the House of Commons to stop the chancellor of the exchequer, Sir John Simon, making a statement on the British position until the conference idea had been discussed. The outcome, expressed in a Foreign Office note later filed in the prime minister's papers, was unequivocal:

The reply, I think, to Italy shd be that we have already told Germany that she must immediately withdraw her troops from Poland if we are not to come to the assistance of Poland, and by that condition we stand. We could not contemplate urging Poland to agree to a Conference with German troops still on Polish soil.[38]

After further phone calls to Bonnet, who pressed the idea of the conference forcefully on his British counterpart, Halifax finally rang Ciano at 6.38 in the evening to tell him that German withdrawal was a requirement, as was the restoration of Danzig's status as a free city. Ciano finally let it be known at 9.30 that he and Mussolini had abandoned the idea altogether. 'It seems to me that nothing else is to be done,' wrote Ciano later in his diary. 'It is not our business to give Hitler advice of this nature that he would reject with decisiveness, perhaps with contempt.'[39] In Italy the realization that the coming war would not involve Italian participation in any form was welcomed with relief. Mussolini had to ban a peace demonstration in the Piazza Venezia, in the heart of Rome. 'The usual pacifists,' Mussolini complained.[40] 'One can continue to live,' wrote the anti-fascist jurist Piero Calamandrei in his diary on 2 September, 'one can continue to take walks in the woods, to paint, to sleep in one's bed.'[41] The following day Hitler sent Mussolini a letter thanking him for his intervention and explaining that no conference was possible that devalued the 'blood sacrifice' already made by German soldiers.[42] On 5 September the Italian press finally published the news that Mussolini had heroically tried to intervene on the side of peace but had been frustrated by British intransigence: 'The Duce,' ran the headline, 'has tried right to the very last moment to save the peace of Europe.'[43]

There is no doubt that the combination of Mussolini's intervention, Bonnet's pacifism and the uncertainty about French constitutional requirements created a situation of some confusion for Halifax and Chamberlain, who paid all these issues greater attention than they deserved. At the same time the anxiety generated by the failure to give a firm deadline for the ultimatum preyed on the patience of ministers, members of parliament and the public, who wanted an end to the tension. Unable to decide what should be broadcast that day, the BBC played gramophone records interrupted by occasional news bulletins.[44]

What followed during the late afternoon and evening was a government crisis quite out of proportion to the reality of the situation. At 4.30 in the afternoon the British cabinet met and asked for a firm deadline to be given. Halifax and Chamberlain insisted that the final decision still rested with the French, but as Halifax later put it, 'the Cabinet itself was in an extremely difficult mood.'[45] The chiefs of staff were present, and all insisted that an ultimatum must be given sooner rather than later. Hore-Belisha argued that if the Germans had been prepared to consider Ciano's proposal, 'it showed that they were weakening', and he recommended an ultimatum deadline of midnight, which was finally agreed by the cabinet at 5 p.m.[46] But by the time Halifax and Chamberlain were due to address the House of Lords and the House of Commons respectively they had failed to change the French view that an ultimatum should not expire for a further 48 hours. As a result the statements made shortly after 7.30 still gave no time limit. Halifax found little problem in the Lords, which accepted his assurances that as soon as talks with the French were concluded a definite time would be put for a German answer. He returned home and dressed for a dinner engagement. Chamberlain, by contrast, found a chamber in a state of anxious and truculent expectation.

The scene that followed is often regarded as a turning point in the countdown to war. The House had been sitting all afternoon debating, at times rancorously, a whole number of emergency bills for the expected war. At around 6 o'clock the sitting was suspended, to await

Chamberlain's announcement. 'Everyone was restless,' wrote Edward Spears in his diary. 'Few sat in the Chamber. Men moved from group to group, in the smoking room, on the terrace, back to the lobbies.'[47] Impatience mounted when they were called back to the chamber at 7 only to be left there for 45 minutes until Chamberlain finally appeared. The mood, Harold Nicolson recorded, was like 'a court awaiting the verdict of a jury'.[48] Chamberlain's brief four-minute speech was ill-prepared, a sharp contrast with the vigour of his performance the previous evening. He told the House that there were delays because of Ciano's proposed conference, and he explored the idea that if Germany withdrew its forces the government would regard the position as being the same as it was 'before the German forces crossed the Polish frontier'. He concluded by rejecting the German seizure of Danzig as a violation of treaties to which Britain was a party.[49] The speech evoked not a single response from the parliamentary benches. 'Members sat,' Spears wrote, 'as if turned to stone.'[50]

The leader of the Labour opposition, Arthur Greenwood, rose to speak. He was deputizing for Clement Attlee, who was convalescing from a prostate operation. Before Greenwood could begin, the Conservative MP Leo Amery called out, 'Speak for England'. The interruption was not recorded in *Hansard*, the stenographic report of parliamentary debates, as most interjections were, but it appears in a number of eyewitness accounts, so must certainly have taken place. Another Conservative MP, Robert Boothby, later claimed that he had called out, 'You speak for Britain', and it is possible that a number of voices were raised at the same time in the tension of the moment.[51] Greenwood rose to the occasion with a spontaneous eloquence: 'I wonder how long we are prepared to vacillate at a time when Britain and all that Britain stands for, and human civilization are in peril.' He hoped that Chamberlain would have a definite announcement about war or peace on the following morning. As he tried to finish, there were further shouts from the floor of the House. Chamberlain spoke again briefly, trying to allay suspicion that his statement suggested 'any weakening' of the position on Poland, but the debate was made more difficult when the pacifist Labour MP James Maxton immediately got up to express the hope that when Chamberlain came back to the House it would be to say there was 'a definite possibility of saving peace'. On the way out of the chamber, another Labour MP called him a 'bloody pacifist'.[52] 'Drunken lout,' replied Maxton. The House broke up, Leo Amery wrote in his diary, 'in indescribable confusion'. [53]

As soon as the session was over, a group of cabinet members met in the rooms of the chancellor of the exchequer, Sir John Simon, to express their disbelief and anger over the absence of a declaration of war. Simon told Chamberlain, who was still in the House, that his colleagues wanted a definite statement. When Chamberlain returned to No. 10 he telephoned Halifax, who was on the point of going out to dinner, and asked him to come to Downing Street. 'I had never heard the prime minister so disturbed,' Halifax later wrote, and when he arrived he found Chamberlain convinced that his government would fall on the following day without an ultimatum.[54] A letter arrived from Simon and the cabinet rebels again insisting on an early deadline. The French ambassador, Charles Corbin, was summoned and anxious phone calls made to Bonnet, Daladier and Eric Phipps, the ambassador in Paris. Outside, a heavy thunderstorm lent the force of nature to the unfolding drama within. The French side was reluctant to speed things up, and Simon was summoned to No. 10 to tell Corbin that the unity of the British government was in danger of collapsing. A few minutes later, Halifax again called Bonnet, who had been forced by Daladier to agree to the delivery of a French ultimatum the following day. At 11.30 in the evening the British cabinet met again and agreed on an ultimatum to be delivered at 9 the following morning, to expire at 11 a.m. Halifax went to draft the ultimatum at the Foreign Office. In the early hours of the morning he met the Labour politician Hugh Dalton. 'Can you give me any hope?' Halifax recalled being asked. 'If by "hope" you mean hope of being at war, I think I can give you some hope for tomorrow,' he replied. 'Thank God!' responded Dalton. [55]

It is possible to exaggerate the seriousness of the political revolt against Chamberlain, whose commitment to the Polish treaty was constant throughout the days of crisis. Halifax thought the episode 'showed democratic assemblies at their worst'.[56] His undersecretary, Alexander Cadogan, writing to the British ambassador in Paris a few days later, said he always suspected that 'Bonnet was the villain of the piece'.[57] Chamberlain, writing to his sister Ida ten days later, complained how difficult it had been to explain his policy clearly to a chamber that was 'out of hand, torn with suspicions, ready . . . to believe the Govt guilty of any cowardice and treachery'.[58] Chamberlain paid the price of his single-minded pursuit of a European solution; when the crisis came it was difficult for even his own party not to suspect that he might evade a decision which placed him, as one MP put it, in 'moral agony'.[59] Insufficient account is taken in all the final days of the drama of the extraordinary toll imposed on those at the very centre of events that tumbled over each other in bewildering profusion in the course of just a week. Chamberlain by the eve of war was exhausted, though not incapable of action. All of those involved were prey to debilitating bouts of tension, uncertainty and anxiety, and it is little surprise that frayed nerves and hurried thoughts made democratic politics more difficult to conduct in the final days of crisis.

In neither the British nor the French case is there clear evidence that the Polish commitment was to be abandoned in the two days following the German invasion. Even Bonnet, despite his yearning for a peaceful solution, could not publicly state that he wanted to abandon the guarantee to Poland. Nevertheless he strained every nerve in trying to extract a solution that did not involve France going to war. Daladier, on the other hand, while unable to restrain Bonnet, continued as if war were now inevitable. In the early evening of 2 September he addressed the Chamber of Deputies while his deputy spoke to the

Senate, with none of the difficulty suffered by Chamber-lain. The stenographic report of his speech indicates lively applause again and again. He revisited the long story of German aggression, the efforts to save peace and the necessity of honouring the pledge to Poland or else to become 'a France despised, a France isolated, a France discredited'. At the end of his address the deputies rose to their feet and applauded 'lengthily'.[60] The Chamber and Senate unanimously voted 90 billion francs in war credits, the equivalent in Daladier's view to a declaration of war. After the vote, one of the senators, Jacques Bardoux, met the British ambassador, who in a sudden moment of emotion seized him by the hand and exclaimed 'Vive la France!'[61] At the French Foreign Office divisions remained. Fresh reports from French consuls in Germany told of poor German morale, but the reports were capa-ble of being used by both sides, those who wanted to go to war regardless and those who hoped Germany would crack before war came. By the evening, after the parlia-mentary session, war could no longer be avoided: 'everyone is black this evening,' commented one official in his diary. 'War and a long war at that.'[62]

Historians, nevertheless, have generally been unwill-ing to concede that Chamberlain and Daladier were entirely committed to war at this point rather than to further appeasement. This view flies in the face of real-ity. It is surely implausible to suggest that Chamberlain and Daladier would ever have been able to halt the process of war preparations already set in train, or to have defied public opinion so openly. Unlike Hitler, who could order or cancel war at will, Western leaders were part of a complex political machine towards which they had both a responsibility and an obligation. No doubt in both cases there existed a strong desire to try to see to the very last moment what chance there was that the earlier illusions of German vulnerability or German political conflict might after all engender a crisis for Hitler if they held firm. It may well be that Chamberlain in the end needed someone else to push him formally to declare war, so difficult was it to reconcile war with his own worldview; but on the central issue of honouring the pledge to wage war when Poland was attacked there are no solid grounds for arguing he would not have done so.

The Failure of Peace

3 September 1939

Sunday 3 September was the day the world war began. It started, recalled the English novelist Storm Jameson, 'on a day of unusual beauty, clear hot sun, dazzlingly white clouds beneath a blue zenith, a high soft wind'.[1] The illusions on both sides that the other would give way when faced with reality were finally dispelled. The day is always remembered as Chamberlain's day, whereas 1 September had been Hitler's. Against all his better instincts and expectations, Chamberlain found himself compelled to declare a war he had not wanted. Though history has generally found Chamberlain wanting in courage, the final step of making a declaration whose implications were profound and far-reaching was certainly a courageous act. No less courageous, though often overlooked, was the declaration of war made later on the same day by Daladier, whose moral rejection of war had been as powerful as Chamberlain's but who also came to recognize the futility of avoiding a direct confrontation with Hitler's Germany. Democratic leaders had none of the simplicity enjoyed by dictators in choosing war.

By the morning of 3 September the die was cast. The decision to present an ultimatum with a brief time limit had been made late on the previous evening, and nothing happened overnight to change it. Halifax arrived at the Foreign Office at 10 o'clock in the morning but found that 'there was nothing to do'.[2] He was told that Nevile Henderson had delivered the ultimatum as instructed and at 10.50 received yet another phone call from Dahlerus, who suggested that Göring should be invited over at once for a final summit meeting. Cadogan recalled later saying 'Rats!' to Dahlerus; Halifax gave a more considered response, but the meaning was the same.[3] At 11 o'clock Halifax and Cadogan walked to Downing Street to find out the result of the ultimatum. The street was thronged with Londoners; photographs show a generally enthusiastic crowd, full of smiles and Union Jacks. Inside No. 10 the BBC had set up a primitive studio for Chamberlain to broadcast to the nation. By 11.10, ten minutes after the expiry of the British ultimatum, there was no news from Berlin and Chamberlain ordered the service departments to 'consider themselves at war'. Two minutes later came a telephone call from the British Embassy in Berlin confirming that there had indeed been no response from the German side. Chamberlain prepared to make his broadcast. Outside in the corridor Halifax and the prime minister's staff listened through a transmitter set up by BBC engineers.[4]

The broadcast began at 11.15 and lasted only a few minutes. It must certainly have been the most difficult speech of Chamberlain's long career. He had faced the same possibility a year before during the Czech crisis and had drafted a speech to be broadcast in case war broke out on that occasion which began, according to Horace Wilson, 'In spite of all the efforts of His Majesty's Government to maintain peace . . .'[5] The broadcast he made on 3 September was more personal in tone, reflecting the months of psychological struggle he had gone through to reconcile his loathing of war with his readiness to wage it if circumstances dictated: 'You can imagine what a bitter blow it is to me that all my long struggle to win peace has failed.' He revealed that no assurance had been received from Berlin that Hitler would withdraw his forces from Poland 'and that consequently this country is at war with Germany'.[6] It was a brief announcement after weeks of tension and uncertainty, but it was not unexpected. Once it was over, Chamberlain began asking his staff and colleagues how they had liked his performance; he was interrupted by the wail of an air-raid siren. After a brief pause Chamberlain announced, 'That is an air-raid warning'; those present smiled, but Chamberlain repeated his words. In a few moments all those in No. 10, except Halifax's parliamentary secretary, Richard Butler, trooped down to the basement to find the corridor to the underground War Rooms. On the way down they met Mrs Chamberlain with a large basket full of books and gasmasks in case the stay underground was to be a long one. Butler decided he would prefer to die in his own building, and crossed the street to the Foreign Office.[7] The crowds that had gathered outside to greet the prime minister and hear the news of war rushed for shelters and cellars. This was what the popular fear of bombing had led people to expect as soon as war broke out, but it turned out to be a false alarm and after 20 minutes the all-clear sounded. The alarm was attributed to a number of causes – drunken English tourists returning from France in an aeroplane, French officers flying to Britain on official business, RAF aircraft sent on a reconnaissance trip over Heligoland. The Chief of the Air Staff, Sir Cyril Newall, came in person to assure the prime minister that there was nothing to fear.[8]

There were many reactions to Chamberlain's declaration of war. Lord Halifax, a model of British *sang froid*, recalled in a wartime memoir that he had 'seldom felt more moved'. Even critics of Chamberlain found his declaration resolute. Leo Amery, who had triggered the crisis in the House of Commons the night before, thought the broadcast 'good in substance'.[9] Chamberlain's words were aimed principally at the wider British public. It was a warm autumn day after the previous day of rain and storms, a fitting backdrop to the curious sense of relief that some contemporaries recorded once war had been declared. Beatrice Webb, at her cottage in Hampshire, wrote in her diary that evening that she now felt 'detached and calm, the strain has ceased'.[10] Listening to the broadcast in her father's vicarage near Oxford, Penelope Mortimer watched her father stand firmly to attention when afterwards the radio played the national anthem. 'He was fifty-nine,' she recalled, 'and momentarily looked like a young man again, ready for the fight.' In the garden her mother served tea and biscuits to mark the occasion.[11] In another English village, the pacifist Vera Brittain waited for the news with her family. 'Total War now seems inevitable,' she had written in her diary on 1 September. Two days later she sat between her children on a camp bed listening to the radio with tears streaming down her cheeks at the wasted efforts for peace. After the broadcast was finished she went into the nearby woods: 'in the sunny quiet of the gorse and heather, it was impossible to take in the size of the catastrophe.'[12]

The greatest impact was on Chamberlain himself. The strain of having to declare a war he abhorred cannot be underestimated. During the Munich debate in the House of Commons on 6 October 1938, he had reflected on what the responsibility meant to him of weighing peace and war: 'Anybody who had been through what I had to go through day after day, face to face with the thought that in the last resort it would have been I, and I alone, who would have to say that yes or no which would decide the fate of millions of my countrymen – a man who had gone through that could not readily forget.'[13] Similar sentiments assailed him a year later, on 3 September. A week after the outbreak of war he wrote to his sister Ida that the 'days of stress and strain' had made him lose all sense of time; 'life,' he continued, 'is just one long nightmare.' The declaration had nonetheless given Chamberlain too a sense of relief. Apart from one sleepless night, he told his sister, 'the tension has actually decreased'.[14] The relief was visible to members of parliament when Chamberlain arrived at midday, shortly after his broadcast, 'smiling and well', according to one MP. The House, another member recorded, was also 'relaxed and serene'; the strain of the previous day of drama had evaporated, although the opposition refused to cheer when Chamberlain entered the chamber.[15] Chamberlain gave a brief five-minute statement announcing the declaration of war, but before the session closed two pacifist members of parliament were given the floor to denounce the decision to fight. The independent socialist MP John McGovern told the House that he could not support it: 'I do not regard it as being idealistic. I do not regard it as being for freedom, justice and human right. I regard it . . . as a hard, soulless, grinding materialist struggle for human gain.'[16]

A different drama was played out in Berlin, where the German leadership, uncertain to the very last of British and French intentions, found themselves confronting a world war that Hitler had continued to insist would not really materialize. The instructions to Nevile Henderson to deliver an ultimatum in person at the German Foreign Office arrived at 5 o'clock in the morning, although Hitler had already been alerted to expect an ultimatum by a secret telegram from the German embassy in London, delivered late the previous evening. A little before 9 o'clock Henderson entered the building to find only Hitler's chief interpreter, Paul Schmidt. They stood awkwardly opposite each other while Henderson read out the short ultimatum. Schmidt then hurried to the Reich chancellery building, where he found an anxious bevy of waiting officials and soldiers. Ushered into the presence of Hitler and Ribbentrop, Schmidt slowly read out the ultimatum. 'When I finished,' wrote Schmidt in his memoirs, 'there was complete silence. Hitler sat immobile, gazing before him.' After a few moments Hitler turned to Ribbentrop with a savage look and asked, 'What now?'[17]

Hitler was faced with the prospect of a major European war which he had hoped to avoid but which he had not considered entirely unavoidable. There is a sense in which, like Chamberlain, Hitler waited for someone else to take the decision so that the other would take both the responsibility and, later, the blame. It was nevertheless, as his press chief Otto Dietrich recalled, 'plain to see how stunned he was'.[18] He had believed Ribbentrop's many assurances that Britain would not fight, because he wanted to believe them. Exactly what he thought about the outcome cannot be known, but during the course of the day he came back to the view he had expressed earlier: neither Britain nor, in particular, France would fight a full war. When Joseph Goebbels first arrived at the chancellery he found Hitler infuriated by the British stance, determined to fight. A long memorandum denouncing British bellicosity and rejecting the ultimatum, prepared in advance in the German Foreign Office, was to be handed to British officials. 'The German Government and the German people,' ran the document, 'refuse to receive, accept or fulfil the demands in the ultimatum from the British Government.' Ribbentrop telephoned the British embassy at 11.20, asking them to come and fetch the German reply, by which time war had already been declared.[19] A little later Hitler dictated to his air force adjutant, Nicolaus von Below, an appeal to the German people. There was no shorthand-typist present and von Below scribbled down Hitler's words with difficulty. The announcement was immediately taken by Goebbels and broadcast on German radio, alongside broadcasts to Party members, the troops in the east and the troops defending Germany's western frontier.[20] But by the evening Hitler's tone had altered once again. Before he left on his private train, heading for the German–Polish border, he told Goebbels that he still thought Britain and France would only fight a *Kartoffelkrieg*,* not a real campaign.[21] According to Albert Speer, who had been summoned to the chancellery along with others from Hitler's circle so that he could take his leave of them, no one outside took any notice of their new warlord as he left in a fleet of black cars to go through the blacked-out streets to his train, 'in keeping,' Speer thought, 'with the desolate mood'.[22]

Once the general war had arrived there was no question of German troops being pulled back from Poland. Göring was told of Chamberlain's broadcast at 11.45 by Paul Körner, his state secretary. Dahlerus, who was with him, noted that he heard the news 'with visible sorrow', but immediately blamed the British for failing

* Literally a 'potato-war', a metaphor for a war of economic blockade.

to recognize the possibility of a German–British under-standing.[23] After Hitler's departure for the front, Goebbels met Göring in the evening in Berlin. The field marshal told Goebbels that he thought France still showed signs of hesitation. It was, he thought, difficult to tell whether there would be a long war or not. The problem lay with the German people and whether they would put up with war.[24] During the course of the day it was evident that the declaration of war had had a sobering effect on the German public. Shortly after the British ultimatum expired, extra editions of the major German newspapers appeared on the streets announcing that England (they seldom used the term Great Britain) had declared a state of war after the ultimatum had been rejected. The decla-ration was announced over street loudspeakers in Berlin, where William Shirer watched people listen attentively and then stand stunned and unmoving. He wandered through the city, soaked in early autumn sunshine, and read 'astonishment, depression' on the faces of the popu-lation. There were no demonstrations, 'no cheering, no throwing of flowers, no war fever'. Shirer went to the Adlon Hotel, near the Brandenburg Gate, where he met officials from the British Embassy, who shocked him with their insouciance: 'They seemed completely unmoved by events,' he wrote in his diary. 'Talked about *dogs* and stuff.'[25]

The French declaration of war had something of an anti-climax about it in Berlin, since it was assumed that after the British declaration France would follow suit. In the end the gap between the British and French ultimatums was narrower than the French government and military leadership had wanted. After the arguments in the French cabinet on the evening of 2 September, Bonnet was compelled against his will, at midnight, to telegram the French ambassador to expect instructions the following morning to deliver a note at midday, 3 September, demanding a response to the earlier request for a German withdrawal from Poland. Bonnet hoped to postpone the deadline of the new demand to 5 p.m. on 4 September, in case there was one more slim chance of peace. Even then he could not bring himself to declare war; the ambassador was instructed at 10.50 in the morning simply to say that if Germany refused to respond, the French government would be obliged 'to fulfil . . . the commitments that France has contracted towards Poland'.[26] When Coulondre telephoned Paris to ask what constituted German rejection, Bonnet told him to change the time of the deadline to 5 p.m. on 3 September. The change was prompted by Daladier that morning, who had finally received assurances from the French army and navy that an earlier declaration of war was acceptable.[27] Bonnet recalled in his memoirs that he struggled to the end to extract more time in case at the very last moment Hitler would back down. 'I fought for peace,' he later wrote, in defence of his persistent appeasement, 'as one fights to save a sick man while he has a breath left in him.'[28]

At midday, an hour after the British declaration of war, the French ambassador arrived at the German Foreign Office. He was greeted by the state secretary,

Ernst von Weizsäcker, who told him that he was not in a position to answer the question of whether German forces would be withdrawn from Poland or not. Since Coulondre had to deliver his message, he insisted that he be allowed to see Ribbentrop. He was led to the Reich chancellery, where Ribbentrop met him at 12.30. He told Coulondre that a French declaration would constitute an 'aggressive war', but he did not answer the question of whether German troops would be withdrawn. Only after the ambassador asked if his response was negative did Ribbentrop reply, 'Yes'. Coulondre then read out the note announcing that France would honour its obligations to Poland from 5 p.m. that evening.[29] In Paris emergency newspaper editions were already on the street, announcing, 'War: England in a state of war with Germany: since 11.00 this morning!' There were rumours that Hitler was about to back down after all; nurses could be heard shouting to passing soldiers, '*Bonne guerre!*'[30] Provincial prefects reported a mood, as one put it, 'something between resolution and resignation'. Jacques Bardoux recalled in his memoirs that the people of Paris in that moment had an attitude 'of moderation and simplicity, of silence and firmness'; here, as in Berlin, the cheering crowds of 1914 were absent.[31] Shortly before the ultimatum expired, André Maurois, who had been seconded with other academics and literati to a new Committee of Information the day before ('the conversation was brilliant, the disorder terrifying,' he recalled), was seated with a friend in an office, waiting for the fateful hour. 'When the five strokes rang out,' he wrote, 'we clasped each other's hands.'[32] Daladier broadcast to the nation as Chamberlain had done earlier in the day. His appeal was rhetorical and patriotic, where Chamberlain's had been soaked in pathos: 'We are at war because we have had it imposed on us. Each of us is at his post, on the soil of France, in the land of liberty where respect for human dignity finds one of its last refuges.'[33]

The outbreak of a European war provoked a flurry of activity worldwide. The French declaration of war involved their empire automatically, but the British declaration was only on behalf of British colonies and protectorates. During the day other parts of the British Commonwealth made their declarations. The different time-zones meant that Australia and New Zealand declared war late in the evening of 3 September, the government of India late in the afternoon.[34] In Poland the German bombing did not stop people from going on to the streets, anxious for news. Early in the morning, on his way to Lublin, Zygmunt Klukowski, called up as a Polish army doctor, found a bustle of activity everywhere. 'Everyone is waiting for England and France to declare war,' he wrote in his journal, 'But when?' Finally at lunchtime Polish radio broadcast a communiqué to announce that Britain had declared war and France would follow in a few hours; the three national anthems were played. Outside, Klukowski found delighted crowds; within minutes the streets were decorated with the flags of the three nations, held in readiness for the moment Poland's allies became belligerents.[35] In Warsaw a large crowd gathered outside the British embassy to cheer the coming of war once the news had broken, but the greatest celebration was reserved for the French declaration in the afternoon. The French ambassador, Léon Noël, later wrote that before 5 o'clock a large crowd began to gather, drawn from every sector of Polish society. They left flowers and letters at the embassy gates and sang verses of the *Marseillaise*. As the street began to fill to overflowing it was difficult to move. They were, Noël recalled, 'indescribable scenes'. At that moment thousands of Poles believed that their allies would soon be fighting gun for gun, as they were.[36]

The most urgent action to be taken concerned military policy. In Berlin, Hitler signed Directive No. 2, which called for a defensive posture in the west and permitted the initial stages of the naval war, with instructions to lay mines and attack merchant shipping, both requested earlier by the German navy's commander-in-chief, Admiral Erich Raeder.[37] The navy high command took a generally pessimistic view of German prospects. After hearing of the British declaration of war, 'which, according to the Führer's previous assertions, we had no need to expect before about 1944', Raeder wrote down his reflections on the prospects for his fleet: 'they can do no more than to show that they know how to die gallantly.'[38] In France the mobilization of six million troops continued, with forward units moving into assigned positions along the Maginot Line of defences facing the German frontier. Troops throughout French North Africa were also on high alert in case Mussolini decided to change his mind about belligerency.

In Britain mobilization had been slower during the week before the outbreak of war, but now had to be accelerated. At the Cabinet Office, War Office officials had assembled at 10.30 in the morning to see if war would actually be declared. While they waited, three different telegrams were prepared for use depending on the outcome: one for postponement of war, one for a declaration of war from a certain but later hour, one for the immediate outbreak of hostilities. Major-General Kennedy, who had drafted the telegrams, kept a fourth blank piece of paper in case the German side did something unexpected.[39] Just before Chamberlain's radio broadcast they were told to send version three, the War Telegram, to all service chiefs. In the subsequent confusion caused by the air-raid alarm, no one thought to send the news to the war minister, who had to wait until lunchtime before he was certain that hostilities had actually begun. Great confusion was caused by the fact that no decision had yet been made about who was to command the British war effort as commander-in-chief of the British Expeditionary Force. After a difficult meeting of Chamberlain's first War Cabinet at 5 p.m., in which Churchill now sat as First Lord of the Admiralty, it was agreed that the command should be given to General Gort, while his role as Chief of the Imperial General Staff would be taken by General Ironside, despite fears voiced in the cabinet discussion that he was an unreliable intriguer.[40] Both men were presented to the king at 7.30 in the evening, and British forces finally had a settled high command.

Most of the military action was confined to the Polish front. On 3 September forces from German Army Group North succeeded in bridging the Polish Corridor and establishing a link with East Prussia. German Army Group South under General Gerd von Rundstedt made continuous progress towards Cracow and Łódź, with Walter von Reichenau's Tenth Army seizing Czestochowa, in between the two major cities. The German air force bombed targets far in the rear and made it difficult for Polish forces to regroup as they retreated. In the Gulf of Danzig the German navy sank the Polish minelayer *Gryf* and the destroyer *Wicher* while bombarding the Polish port of Gdynia.[41] German commanders were already confident of defeating the Polish forces quickly, while the Polish command recognized the impossibility of their position. Although no definite promises had been made by British or French commanders that they would assist Poland immediately, Poland's leaders hoped that something would be done to relieve the pressure. The Royal Air Force dropped six million leaflets over Germany during the course of the day, but otherwise neither of Poland's new allies contributed anything to relieve the remorseless progress of German forces. Two days later, on 5 September, a frustrated British embassy official in Warsaw, Robin Hankey, son of the former cabinet secretary, wrote a furious letter to his father (who had just become a member of Chamberlain's War Cabinet as minister without portfolio) about the failure to help Poland:

But it's time we gave Gerry a bean-load. As seen from here, we aren't pulling any weight at all. The Polski will fight bravely, but he can't take on the Hun all alone. It's *high time* we destroyed Germany's factories. It's all balls about military objectives. They've bombed open towns up and down Poland . . . We *must* go for Germany before the Eastern Front is broken up.[42]

The truth gradually became clear to the Polish leadership: the West had never intended to fight in their defence. Robin's father, Maurice Hankey, drafted a speech later in September in which he remarked that the Poles had known all along that the amount of help they could get from the West would be limited. 'The ultimate rescue of the free peoples,' he wrote, 'gives determination to ourselves and consolation to the Poles.'[43] In the event, Poland was betrayed by war just as Czechoslovakia was betrayed by peace.

Action in the Western theatre was almost non-existent. The fear of bombing as the first act of war between developed states was shown to be unfounded. When Roosevelt had appealed on 1 September to the combatant powers not to engage in the wanton attack of civilians from the air, the British government had responded at once that it was already British policy to confine attacks only to 'strictly military targets' as long as the same self-denying ordinance were observed by other powers. Hitler, too, confirmed that this was also the German position.[44]

Nevertheless, the Air Ministry alerted the Royal Air Force at 2.15 on the morning of 3 September that a state of war would almost certainly exist by 11 a.m. and that attacks should be expected at least two hours earlier than that. Bomber Command was told to stand by to await separate orders 'for operations at present envisaged'. These orders extended in the end to dropping leaflets. The only other emergency measure taken that day was to complete the inflation of barrage balloons, many of which had been in place but not filled with gas until a state of war was declared.[45] The only serious action was not in the air, but at sea. During the evening the 13,500-ton British liner *Athenia* was torpedoed by the German submarine U-30 some 200 miles west of the Scottish Hebrides Islands, because the commander mistook the liner, with around 1,500 passengers and crew on board, for an auxiliary cruiser. A total of 128 people lost their lives, 28 of them American. Four vessels in the vicinity, including one Norwegian, responded to the SOS call and rescued most of those on board. The ship finally sank at 10.40 the following morning. At first the German navy did not believe the reports, since German submarines were under strict instructions not to attack civilian vessels. Hitler ordered a denial to be published, but it was discovered when U-30 returned to port that her captain, Lieutenant Lemp, had indeed ordered the sinking. He claimed he had done so in a moment of excitement following the opening of his sealed orders after the declaration of war. He and his crew were sworn to secrecy, and Lemp died when his next submarine was sunk in May 1941. Hitler sent out special orders to naval units that on no account were passenger liners to be attacked, but this stipulation lasted only a further year.[46]

The evening of 3 September was calm in the two Western states after the weeks of escalating tension. 'Like a swimmer tired of battling with a contrary current,' wrote the British journalist Malcolm Muggeridge, 'abandoning the struggle, and letting himself be carried along by what he had long tried to resist, this last crisis was left to take its course.'[47] Some of those intimately bound up in the crisis relaxed as their work for peace came to an end. Cadogan took his wife for a tour of the Foreign Office War Rooms in the afternoon, and then went for a walk in Buckingham Palace gardens with Halifax. After several almost sleepless nights he returned home at 7.30 for dinner and bed, writing in his diary that now 'there is relief; doubts resolved', only to be woken again by an air-raid alarm at 3 in the morning.[48] In the evening King George VI broadcast to the British Empire. He had decided that day to keep a diary for the first time in order to mark the transition to war. In his first entry he recalled his own feelings as a young midshipman when war broke out in 1914 and then added 'those of us who had been through the Great War never wanted another . . .'[49] Bonnet, after seeing the German chargé d'affaires at 7.30 in the evening to convey formally the existence of a state of war, wrote in his daily journal about his failure to understand his colleagues who preferred war to peace; the final part of the entry was later torn up.[50] In a small English village in Norfolk, a shopworker, keeping a diary for the British Mass Observation organization, wrote in the evening that she found it hard to imagine that her male friends would shortly be called up: 'Decide to think of them as killed off,' she wrote, 'and then it will not be such a blow if they are, and will be a great joy if at the end they are not.'[51]

Long after Europeans had retired to sleep, President Roosevelt broadcast to the American people pledging their country to neutrality. 'There will be no blackout of peace in the United States,' he told them. Earlier that day he had met with his cabinet and advisers to discuss the breakout of a war he had hoped might be averted. The gloomy gathering, wrote Adolf Berle, assistant secretary-of-state, was the 'last meeting of the death watch over Europe'.[52]

In Germany the atmosphere was sombre at last. Germans who wanted to hear for themselves the news of what was happening were banned from listening to any news except German news. A decree had come into force signed by Hitler two days before prohibiting the population from listening to foreign radio broadcasts; in the worst cases those who endangered state security were to be subject to capital punishment, in other cases to periods of imprisonment.[53] Those who had been critical of Hitler's strategy also had to be more circumspect. In the evening the army chief of staff, General Franz Halder, talked of his fears to a fellow officer. 'He was deeply serious,' recorded Colonel Liss. '"Now the English too," he said, "the Englishman is tenacious. Now it will last a long time."'[54] Weizsäcker, who had hoped to influence

Ribbentrop and secure peace, confided to his diary his hope that the war would not completely destroy 'everything that is good and valuable'.[55] In the evening, Birger Dahlerus, disillusioned by the failure of his shuttle diplomacy, was visited at his hotel by Göring's state secretary, who came to thank him for all his efforts for peace. The following morning he saw Göring for the last time, who told him he hoped that, after the rapid conquest of Poland, the Western states would recognize that the conflict 'should be settled as soon as possible, and a world war avoided'.[56] That same day the British and French embassy staffs were loaded into two Pullman trains and sent back to their capitals, as was their right under international law.

Conclusion
Why War?

Why did a general European war break out in September 1939? There was much talk in the days of crisis about the lessons of the outbreak of war in 1914. It was widely assumed in the West that the muddled diplomacy that produced war twenty-five years before would not be responsible for explaining war in 1939. In his letter to Hitler on 22 August 1939 Chamberlain insisted that he did not want to repeat 1914, when 'the great catastrophe would have been avoided' if the British government had made its position clearer. In telling Hitler plainly that Britain would fight for Poland, he continued, he wanted to avoid any 'tragic misunderstanding'.[1] In a wartime note on British foreign policy, Lord Halifax argued that he thought Hitler might have been deterred 'if, as we had failed to do in 1914, we made it unmistakably clear that the particular acts of aggression which he was believed to have in mind, would result in general war'.[2] When Hitler attacked Poland, Britain and France duly honoured their pledge to defend Poland's independence and war resulted.

Although in simple terms this explains exactly why war broke out, the reality was far more complex. Even the hope that no one would be able to compare 1914 with 1939 came under critical scrutiny later in the war, when the British historian Sir Llewellyn Woodward was invited to begin to write an official survey of British foreign policy before the outbreak of war. Woodward wrote to Halifax in 1943 asking him to check thoroughly an early proof of what he had written. After the experience of the post mortem on 1914, wrote Woodward, he felt sure that 'the Germans will again apply their pedantic literalism to every scrap of evidence about the origins of this war. Hence we ought to leave no gaps for the German type of "higher critic".'[3] Halifax replied that he had been worried throughout the final days of the crisis that Hitler might produce 'specious terms', which would look reasonable enough but which the Poles would have to reject. In those circumstances, continued Halifax, British support for the Poles might have looked like the notorious German 'blank cheque' given to Austria in 1914, and international opinion would think it was Britain that 'had precipitated war'. Luckily, concluded Halifax, Hitler invaded Poland and the dilemma never arose.[4]

If Hitler was responsible for war in 1939, this still begs the larger question of what kind of war he wanted. Few historians now accept that Hitler had any plan or blueprint for world conquest, in which Poland was a stepping stone to some distant German world empire. Indeed recent research has suggested that there were almost no plans for what to do with a conquered Poland and that the vision of a new German empire in central and eastern Europe had to be improvised almost from scratch.[5] The key difficulty is to determine whether Hitler wanted a local war against Poland in 1939, as he always insisted, or whether he decided at some point in 1939 to turn on the West instead, and have a general European war. There is an argument to be made that Hitler was pressed into accepting a war with Britain and France because of the growing costs of rearmament, the difficulty of meeting the trade requirements to fuel further military build-up and a realization that Germany's temporary lead in armaments might soon evaporate. 'Hitler's decision to unleash a general European war', as one historian has recently put it, was a case of 'better sooner than later'.[6] Behind the decision to launch a general war, it has been claimed, lay larger ambitions for a contest for world power with the United States, which Hitler saw as the instrument of a world Jewish conspiracy.[7] These arguments privilege the West too much. Hitler's ambition for conquest in the East was consistent with much German geopolitical fantasy going back decades, and Hitler was as absorbed as any provincial central European German nationalist might be with the idea of carving out from Eastern Europe a larger and more savage version of the Habsburg Empire, armed with a new model of economic exploitation (the so-called 'large area economy') and nourished on dreams of a racial utopia. Hitler wanted the war with Poland to flesh out the central European empire and open the way for the eventual confrontation with Stalin's Soviet Union.[8]

The second problem with the argument that Hitler wanted general war is the nature of the evidence. In his testamentary conversations recorded by Martin Bormann in the last weeks of the Second World War, Hitler complained that 'it is untrue, that I or anyone else in Germany wanted to have the [general] war in the year 1939.'[9] Although Hitler is scarcely a reliable witness in his own defence, the evidence of the last weeks before the outbreak of war shows him again and again repeating to those around him in the political and military elite that he wanted to localize the conflict. His favourite architect and party colleague, Albert Speer, wrote in his memoirs that Hitler 'stuck unswervingly to his opinion that the West was too feeble, too worn out, and too decadent to begin the war seriously'. Speer thought that Hitler for some time after 3 September was still not fully aware 'that he had irrevocably unleashed a world war'.[10] There was a high element of risk, as Hitler himself recognized, but by August 1939 he had persuaded himself that Poland was an enemy that deserved to be conquered and punished, and he failed to understand what business it was of Britain and France to become involved. This view he shared with a great many in the German population, who could see the sense of a war to settle the outstanding issues with the Poles, whose state was regarded as an illegitimate offspring of the despised Versailles settlement, but could see no sense in a war with the West. Even this more limited ambition had an essential irrationality, since the 'free hand in the east' that Hitler wanted was a chimera. The invasion of Poland brought Germany face to face with a rapidly arming colossus whose communist leaders had no intention of permitting a free hand to Hitler or anyone else. Hitler's decision for war with Poland was taken not because he wanted to fight the West – which he could have done simply by declaring war – but because of his conviction that in a battle of wills between the two sides, his would prevail and the West would recoil. As Nicolaus von Below described it in his memoirs, Hitler took the risk while 'in the depths of his being hoping against hope that Britain would step back from the brink'.[11]

The more difficult thing to explain is why Britain and France, having apparently conceded so much in the 1930s to the ambitions of the three Axis states, Germany, Italy and Japan, chose to fight over Poland in 1939. The simple answer here, of course, is that Poland in defying Hitler accepted war; and because Polish independence had been guaranteed in March 1939, Britain and France had an obligation to fight Germany as well. But Britain and France had many problems to overcome in bringing their military preparations in line with their ambitions, not least the onset of serious economic and financial constraints as rearmament reached top gear in 1939. It was also necessary to reconcile the prospect of war with populations a large part of whom had been strongly anti-war throughout the years of international crisis. The costs of waging a major war which risked the future of the British and French empires, and their status as great powers, has provoked in recent years a reassessment of the wisdom of going to war at all. The fight against Hitler can be seen to have been, as the American politician Patrick Buchanan recently described it, 'an unnecessary war'. According to Buchanan the war cost the British their empire and created the conditions for fifty years of Cold War and communist domination of Eastern Europe and Asia. The greatest mistake was the guarantee to Poland, which made a war inevitable. 'What Chamberlain's war guarantee wrought,' writes Buchanan, 'was the bloodiest war in all of history.'[12]

This is a view that takes almost no account of the circumstances of the time. Britain and France did not opt for war in 1939 because they wanted to unleash Armageddon. Indeed everything about British and French efforts first to appease, then to deter, Germany was intended to avoid instigating a second Great War in Europe. Deterrence in the end failed, but the obverse of every strategy to deter is the willingness to use force. Britain and France did not choose war by giving a 'war guarantee', for both hoped that the sight of two heavily armed states, with access to greater economic resources and military potential, would force Hitler's hand even on the very edge of war. Alexander Cadogan wrote in his diary around midnight on 31 August, as German troops grabbed a few more hours of sleep before moving to their battle-stations, 'But it *does* seem to me Hitler is hesitant and trying all sorts of dodges, including last-minute bluff.'[13]

The British and French decision for war has also to be

seen against the background of growing fears in both populations that Germany in particular represented a profound threat to their existing way of life and the values that they wished to see observed in the conduct of international affairs. Although it is often argued, and with justice, that neither state cared very much to observe those values in the treatment of their empires, the two powers saw themselves as self-appointed guardians of a Western world assailed by internal anxiety and external threat. In Britain in particular there existed a strong sense of responsibility for keeping the wider world in order. 'Great Britain,' wrote the politician Oliver Harvey in April 1939, in a wide-ranging survey of the international order, 'is the greatest, richest and potentially strongest Power,' and should use that power to restore sanity to the world.[14] In a speech the same year, Lord Halifax reminded his audience 'that this country and the great political society of which it is the origin and a centre has an immense responsibility and that its strength is the best guarantee the world can have . . .'.[15] This sense that Britain might play the role of what Halifax called 'a Moral High Commissioner' was an element in Britain's self-perception that informed much of the rhetoric used to confront Hitler in 1939. After the war had broken out, when Britain and France had manifestly failed to do justice to Poland, Halifax gave a speech in January 1940 returning to the theme that the Allied war was not about Poland at all, but involved nothing less than 'the liberty and independence of our own country and commonwealth, and of all European states'.[16]

The popular view saw the contest less as a struggle of ideological orders, but it was nevertheless coloured by hostility to fascism and militarism and a demonization of Hitler as the architect of crisis. An Englishwoman working in a fish-and-chip shop, writing for Mass Observation, recorded the views of her customers on the day Germany invaded Poland: 'We've got to stop him now'; 'Bloody well stop him'; 'Put him on an island like the Kaiser' (a curiously conflated recollection of Napoleon and Wilhelm II); 'Blooming devil, we can't let him do that can we?'[17] All of these sentiments were directed at Hitler rather than the Germans, but they reflect a growing readiness evident in Britain throughout the summer months to accept the necessity for war. One British observer reported to the Foreign Office in late July that there was a growing belief among Germans too 'that a very large number of people in this country really do want a war against them'.[18] In France there was a greater hostility to German aggression than simply to fascism or Hitler. After the outbreak of war the French government asked their British ally if it was possible to distinguish less obviously between 'Nazis' and 'Germans' in discussing war aims, since in France it was the war against Germany, for the third time in seventy years, that stoked public determination to fight.[19] André Maurois recalled that on 31 August his barber repeated the phrase made popular that autumn: '*Il faut en finir!*', 'It must be finished with'. Maurois then wrote his article for *Le Figaro* in which he talked not of the threat of Hitlerism, but 'the menace of Germany'.[20] Popular endorsement in

September 1939, coloured even though it was with regret, anxiety and resentment, saw the conflict as a 'necessary war'.

Nevertheless, the wider framework for explaining war in 1939 implies an inevitability that makes the last days of drama less significant than they actually were. The final crisis was not entirely scripted in advance. As in 1914 the protagonists argued, manoeuvred, postured and calculated; as in 1914 they did so with partial information, ambiguous intelligence and blind conviction. It is not impossible that different decisions might have been taken at moments in the crisis because of factors generated by the heightened tension itself, as evidenced by Hitler's decision to cancel invasion on 25 August, or the Polish willingness to negotiate, or the complex hostility between Bonnet and Daladier. All aggravated international crises, from the Crimean War to the invasion of Iraq, have generated short-term periods of unstable political interaction and unpredictable circumstance before the onset of hostilities. The last ten days before the outbreak of war were a characteristic example of high-risk confrontation.

The first element each protagonist had to face was a growing mental and physical exhaustion in the face of events that moved so swiftly that they threatened to overwhelm those who confronted them. Hitler was, according to Speer, 'in an unwonted state of nerves' in the last days of August, giving the impression that he was 'exhausted from overwork'.[21] Goebbels complained day after day in his diary that he retired to sleep late: 'Late to bed, out early,' on 23 August; two days later, 'Late and dead tired, a few hours sleep'; 'three o'clock at night still in the office . . . a few hours sleep', on 26 August; and so on.[22] In London, Cadogan penned very similar entries after returning home in the early hours of every morning: 'mad with fatigue', on 30 August; 'can't give full or connected account, too tired', on the following night.[23] Neville Chamberlain gave an account of his state of mind in a letter written to his sister Hilda on 27 August that conveys the sense of perpetual tension under which all the major players operated:

Phew! What a week. One or two more like this one would take years off my life. Whether this be a war of nerves only or just the preliminary stages of a real war it takes very strong nerves to stand it and retain one's sanity and courage. I feel like a man driving a clumsy coach over a narrow crooked road along the face of a precipice. You hardly dare to look down lest you should turn giddy . . .[24]

Many eye-witnesses in the last days before war attest to the strain apparent on Chamberlain's face. Chamberlain was anxious to be involved in everything he could, which left him with a punishing schedule for a man of seventy. When the chiefs of staff asked him on 30 August to arrange a meeting to discuss plans for the opening of hostilities, Chamberlain scribbled on the note, 'It is difficult to fix appointments ahead just now.'[25] The capacity to control events in such a situation became increasingly attenuated. The sense of 'events taking over', as those involved grew more steadily subject to the mental pressures and physical debilitation of long periods of intense labour with little sleep, made it increasingly difficult to think in any terms outside the immediate crisis of the moment or to consider the larger consequences.

The narrowing of vision generated by the conditions of crisis provoked a growing irrationality in which the wider picture or the longer causes of the confrontation were abandoned in favour of a restricted 'mental box' in which decisions had now to be made. In Germany the framework for the crisis was Hitler's determination to punish the Poles for all their alleged transgressions and the conviction that the West would back down. Every shred of intelligence information, including the numerous intercepts by the German intelligence service of telephone and cipher messages back to London and Paris, was examined from this point of view, not to confound the conviction but to make it firmer. In London and Paris the obsession with the deterrent effect of firmness again brought every piece of intelligence information and every communication from Germany under the spotlight, with the hope of detecting in the phrases used or words chosen some hint that Hitler might back down. The irrational nature of that expectation was seldom confronted in the final days. At the British Foreign Office, Richard Butler wrote down the ways out of the crisis as he saw it on the eve of war. Either 'Hitler falls on the Poles with his ready mobilized army and general war results'; or, 'He forfeits his wish to destroy the Poles, pockets his pride and sends his army home.'[26] In the cold light of day the second of these options now seems fantastic, but it was the hope in London and Paris right up to the end of peace.

The narrow mental box on each side contained its own moral universe. Hitler and his senior political colleagues almost certainly convinced themselves that the war against Poland was entirely justified on moral terms, however criminal the actual plans for war. Each act of Polish 'atrocity' was then used to justify the central focus on solving the Polish question at all costs, rather than placing it in a more rational framework for possible compromise or assessing the likely results of precipitate action. On the British and French side the search for a justification that had an immediate meaning was found in the concept of honour. Maintaining the guarantee to Poland at all costs was the alternative to national dishonour, and although this might seem a moral commitment too old-fashioned for the diplomacy of 1930s Europe, it was repeated regularly in the final days of crisis and above all in the interim between the invasion of Poland and the declaration of war. It had a simplicity that cut through all the other arguments surrounding the justification or otherwise for launching war, and narrowed the moral outlook of the democracies to a single word. When Arthur Greenwood hesitated at the end of his speech on the evening of 2 September in the search for a word to describe what was at stake, a heckler called out 'Honour!' Greenwood continued: 'Let me finish my sentence. I was about to say imperilling the foundations of our national honour.'[27] In France, Paul Reynaud recorded in his memoirs the arguments with Bonnet before the declaration of war. In this moment, he wrote, 'one had to choose honour above dishonour', because the path of dishonour would have left an isolated, repudiated France, cut off from the Anglo-Saxon world, at the risk of a quick defeat by a triumphant Germany.[28] As it turned out, in 1940 honour produced the same outcome as dishonour.

The search for a convincing and temporary moral claim during the crisis did not make war completely inevitable, but it made it hard to avoid. The battle of wills in the last days of peace, chiefly between two utterly contrasting protagonists, Hitler and Chamberlain, assumed its own dimension independent to a large extent of the long history of military, economic and political events that had brought them to the impending confrontation in the first place. The final decisions had a rare immediacy. But once the decisions had been made the narrow framework gave way once more to a broader assessment of possibilities. Hitler again became convinced that Britain and France would not seriously fight once Poland was beaten and divided between Germany and the Soviet Union, while Britain and France had to decide more formally exactly what their war aims were beyond satisfying national honour. In late September 1939 the Italian ambassador in Paris visited Sir Eric Phipps, about to retire as British ambassador, to ask him what the Western states thought they would now do. Phipps told him that they would see the war through to victory, even if it took three years. The Italian was surprised by the response. Phipps reported the other's reply in his own words: 'We might fight for years and sacrifice millions of British and French lives, without at the end of even a victorious war being able to re-establish the country we had entered the war to assist. The Russian bear was heavily seated on its part of Poland and would never be dislodged by us.'[29] For all the rhetoric of honour, the reality of war in 1939 was not to save Poland from a cruel occupation but to save Britain and France from the dangers of a disintegrating world.

Notes

PROLOGUE: POLAND, GERMANY AND THE WEST

1. H. G. Wells, *The Shape of Things to Come* (London, 1933), pp. 156–7.
2. *Parliamentary Debates (Hansard)*, Vol. 351, col. 10, 24 August 1939.
3. *Akten zur Deutschen auswärtigen Politik (ADAP)*, Serie D, Band VI (Baden-Baden, 1956), p. 479, Bericht über eine Besprechung am 23 Mai 1939.
4. The National Archives, Kew, London (NA), PREM 1/357, FO memorandum, 'The Polish request for Financial Assistance for military purposes', 9 May 1939, p. 2.
5. C. Kimmich, *The Free City: Danzig and German Foreign Policy, 1919–1934* (New Haven, 1968), pp. 3–9.
6. J. Beck, *Dernier rapport: politique polonaise 1926–1939* (Paris, 1955), p. 187.
7. H. S. Levine, *Hitler's Free City: A History of the Nazi Party in Danzig 1925–1939* (Chicago, 1973), pp. 121–5, 127–38.
8. For the best account see A. Zamoyski, *Warsaw 1920: Lenin's Failed Conquest of Europe* (London, 2008).

9. A. Prazmowska, *Eastern Europe and the Origins of the Second World War* (London, 2000), pp. 137, 144–5.

10. G. Engel, *Heeresadjutant bei Hitler, 1938–1943: Aufzeichnungen des Majors Engel* (Stuttgart, 1974), p. 40.

11. W. J_drzejewicz (ed.), *Diplomat in Berlin 1933–1939: Papers and Memoirs of Józef Lipski, Ambassador of Poland* (New York, 1968), pp. 453–8, Doc. 124, Notes concerning ambassador Lipski's conversation with Reich Minister of Foreign Affairs Ribbentrop, 24 October 1938.

12. J_drzejewicz (ed.), *Diplomat in Berlin*, pp. 482, 582. See too D. Schenk, *Hitlers Mann in Danzig: Albert Forster und die NS-Verbrechen in Danzig-Westpreussen* (Bonn, 2000), pp. 103–4.

13. Lipski papers, pp. 503–4, Doc. 138, memorandum on the conference of senior officials with the Polish Minister of Foreign Affairs.

14. NA, PREM 1/331a, note for Horace Wilson from Col. Hastings Ismay, 31 March 1939, encl. intelligence assessment on Poland; note for Wilson from Ismay, 31 March 1939, encl. report from the Deputy Director of Military Intelligence, 'Germany's intentions regarding DANZIG – 30 March 1939'.

15. NA, PREM 1/331a, memorandum by the Secretary of State, 'Danzig', 5 May 1939, pp. 5, 8.

16. Schenk, *Hitlers Mann in Danzig*, pp. 104–5; *ADAP*, Serie D, Band VI, p. 479.

17. The so-called 'War Plan' for a three-year war was already under discussion in March and was agreed in the British War Cabinet a few days after the outbreak of war. See NA, AIR 9/105, Chief of Staff, 'British Strategical Memorandum', 20 March 1939; PREM 1/377, minute on war aims, 9 September 1939. Planning was to be based 'upon the assumption that the war will last for three years or more'.

18. NA, PREM 1/357, FO memorandum, 'The Polish request for Financial Assistance for military purposes', 9 May 1939; aide memoire from Polish ambassador, 12 May 1939; memorandum for the prime minister from Sir John Simon, 15 May 1939; Simon to Halifax, 24 July 1939.

19. G. Bonnet, *Quai d'Orsay* (Isle of Man, 1965), p. 251; Borthwick Archive, University of York, Halifax papers, A4.410.12/1, 'Foreign Policy 1938–9: an unpublished note' [n.d.], p. 3.

20. H. Michaelis and E. Schraepler (eds.), *Ursachen und Folgen vom deutschen Zusammenbruch 1918 und 1945 bis zur staatlichen Neuordnung Deutschlands in der Gegenwart* (Berlin, n.d.), Vol. xiii, p. 481, Niederschrift über die Aussprache Adolf Hitlers, 22 August 1939. On the fall of Western governments see L. E. Hill (ed.), *Die Weizsdcker-Papiere 1933–1950* (Frankfurt am Main, 1974), p. 159, diary entry for 23 August 1939.

21. NA, PREM 1/331a, R. Makins (FO), 'Record of conversation with M. Burckhardt', 12 June 1939, p. 4.

22. Magdalene College, Cambridge, Inge papers, Vol. 36, diary 1938–9, entry for 16 March 1939.

23. NA, PREM 1/331a, War Office to prime minister, August 1939, encl. 'General Ironside's Report on conditions in Poland, 28 July 1939', p. 3.

24. Franklin D. Roosevelt Library, President's Secretary's File, Box 47, State Department to Roosevelt encl. 'Record of Conversation between Under Secretary of State and Polish ambassador, 9 Aug 1939', p. 3.

25. W. L. Shirer, *Berlin Diary: The Journal of a Foreign Correspondent 1934–1941* (London, 1941), p. 143, entry for 13 August 1939.

TIME RUNNING OUT:
24–26 AUGUST 1939

1. H. Rohde, B. Stegmann and H. Umbreit, *Das Deutsche Reich und der Zweite Weltkrieg*, Band II: *Die Errichtung der Hegemonie auf dem europäischen Kontinent* (Stuttgart, 1979), pp. 101–2; Schenk, *Hitlers Mann in Danzig*, pp. 111–12.

2. Rohde et al., *Das Deutsche Reich und der Zweite Weltkrieg*, Band II, pp. 104–7.

3. E. Fröhlich (ed.), *Die Tagebücher von Joseph Goebbels*, Band 7: *Juli 1939-März 1940* (Munich, 1998), p. 76, entry for 25 August 1939.

4. Ibid., p. 77, entry for 26 August 1939.

5. C. Hartman, *Halder: Generalstabschef Hitlers 1938–1942* (Paderborn, 1991), p, 137.

6. B. Engelmann, *In Hitler's Germany: Everyday Life in the Third Reich* (London, 1988), p. 150.

7. See R. J. Overy, 'Strategic Intelligence and the Outbreak of the Second World War', *War in History*, 5 (1998), pp. 475–6.

8. Churchill College Archive, Cambridge, Christie papers, CHRS 1/29B, 'Notes on Poland', 27 June 1939; C. Andrew, *Secret Service:The Making of the British Intelligence Community* (London, 1985), p. 429.

9. R. Self (ed.), *The Neville Chamberlain Diary Letters*, Vol. 4: *The Downing Street Years 1934–40* (Aldershot, 2005), p. 440, Neville Chamberlain to Ida Chamberlain, 19 August 1939; NA, PREM 1/331a, Halifax to Chamberlain, 19 August 1939.

10. S. Bradford, *King George VI* (London, 1989), p. 303.

11. NA, PREM 1/331a, draft letter from Chamberlain to King George VI, 23 August 1939, pp. 1–2.

12. NA, PREM 1/313, minute for prime minister by Sir

Charles Schuster, 23 August 1939; minute, 'Conference on Emergency Powers (Defence) Bill', 23 August 1939.

13. Churchill College Archive, Hore-Belisha papers, HOBE 5/65, 'Precautionary Measures taken by the War Office, 22–28 August 1939'; HOBE 1/8, Diary 1939, entry for 23 August.

14. Churchill College Archive, Hankey papers, HNKY 10/1, letter from Hankey to Horace Wilson, 24 August 1939.

15. Cmd 6106, 'Documents concerning German–Polish Relations and the Outbreak of Hostilities between Great Britain and Germany, 1939', p. 107, speech by the prime minister, 24 August 1939; pp. 96–8, letter from the prime minister to the German chancellor, 22 August 1939.

16. E. Spears, *Assignment to Catastrophe* (London, 1954), pp. 24–5.

17. R. Boyer de Sainte-Suzanne, *Une politique étrangère: Le Quai d'Orsay et Saint-John Perse à l'épreuve d'un regard: Journal novembre 1938-juin 1940* (Paris, 2000), p. 71, entry for 24 August 1939.

18. P. Jackson, *France and the Nazi Menace: Intelligence and Policy Making 1933–1939* (Oxford, 2000), pp. 379–81; Bonnet, *Quai d'Orsay*, pp. 253–7; minutes of the meeting in P. Reynaud, *La France a sauvé l'Europe* (2 vols., Paris, 1947), Vol. 1, pp. 593–5.

19. R. Genebrier, *La France entre en guerre: Le témoignage du chef de cabinet de Daladier* (Paris, 1982), p. 91.

20. B. Bond (ed.), *Chief of Staff: The Diaries of Lieutenant-General Sir Henry Pownall*, Vol. 1: 1933–1940 (London, 1972), p. 161.

21. Spears, *Assignment to Catastrophe*, p. 22.

22. See R. J. Overy, 'Munich: A Mutilated Victory?', *Diplomacy and Statecraft*, 10 (1999), pp. 191–215.

23. A. Salter, *Personality in Politics: Studies of Contemporary Statesmen* (London, 1947), p. 85.

24. Churchill College Archive, Duff Cooper papers, DUFC 8/1/14, undated draft article, p. 5; Trinity College, Cambridge, Butler papers, F77, 'Chamberlain, a candid portrait', published in the *American Mercury*, 5 November 1939.

25. Salter, *Personality in Politics*, p. 85.

26. Butler papers, G10, 'notes on personalities' [n.d. but *c.* June 1939], pp. 1–2; Halifax papers, A4.410.1/3, draft notes for a speech to the 1900 Club, 21 June 1939, pp. 6, 14.

27. Hankey papers, HNKY 1/7, Diary 1923–1942, entry for 24 August 1939.

28. Hankey papers, HNKY 5/4, Hankey to Halifax, 17 August 1939. On Daladier and French politics in 1939 see J. Wardhaugh, *In Pursuit of the People: Political Culture in France, 1934–39* (London, 2009), pp. 206–12, 227–8.

29. Hore-Belisha papers, HOBE 5/64, notes of a conversation with M. Daladier in Paris, 21 August 1939, p. 2.

30. Z. Klukowski, *Diary from the Years of Occupation 1939–44* (ed. A. and H. Klukowski, Urbana, Ill., 1993), p. 4, entry for 25 August 1939.

31. R. Rhodes James (ed.), *'Chips': The Diary of Sir Henry Channon* (2nd edn, London, 1993), p. 209, entry for 25 August 1939.

32. L. De Salvo and M. A. Leaska (eds.), *The Letters of Vita Sackville-West to Virginia Woolf* (New York, 1985), p. 425, letter of 25 August 1939.

33. Shirer, *Berlin Diary*, p. 148, entry for 24 August 1939.

34. Hill (ed.), *Die Weizsäcker-Papiere*, p. 160, entry for 24 August 1939.

35. Franklin D. Roosevelt Library, Berle papers, Box 64, Stanley Hornbeck to Adolf Berle, 9 June 1939, encl. Memorandum 'Legislation for Peace', p. 6.

36. President's Secretary's Files, Box 31, Thomsen (German embassy) to Cordell Hull, 31 Aug 1939; Kirk (US embassy, Berlin) to Hull, 25 Aug 1939.

37. President's Secretary's Files, Box 31, Memorandum 'Aims and Methods of German Policy', 6 July 1939 [forwarded to the White House by Harold Laski, presented to Roosevelt 25 August].

38. President's Secretary's Files, Box 30, William Bullitt to Roosevelt, 24 Aug 1939; Berle papers, Box 64, Presidential authorisation of ship searches, 28–29 August 1939.

39. President's Secretary's Files, Box 32, Neville Chamberlain to Roosevelt, 25 Aug 1939; Note for the President, 28 Aug 1939; Roosevelt to Chamberlain, 31 Aug 1939.

40. N. von Below, *At Hitler's Side: The Memoirs of Hitler's Luftwaffe Adjutant 1937–1945* (London, 2004), p. 29, entry for 25 August 1939; N. Henderson, *Failure of a Mission: Berlin 1937–1939* (London, 1940), p. 259.

41. Cmd 6106, 'Documents concerning German–Polish Relations', pp. 120–22, Supplementary Communication from the German Chancellor, 25 August 1939.

42. R. De Felice (ed.), *Galeazzo Ciano: Diario 1937–1943* (Milan, 1980), pp. 326–7. Quotation cited in H. J. Burgwyn, *Italian Foreign Policy in the Inter-War Period 1918–1940* (Westport, Conn., 1993), p. 201.

43. S. Colarizi, *La Seconda Guerra Mondiale e la Repubblica* (Turin, 2003), pp. 66–7, 68–70.

44. *Corriere della Sera*, 23 August 1939; *Il Popolo d'Italia*, 23 August 1939.

45. Hill (ed.), *Weizsäcker-Papiere*, pp. 160–61, entry for 25 August 1939. They were almost certainly not on the beach but doubtless wanted to stay out of contact when the news was delivered.

46. Ministère des Affaires Étrangères, *Le Livre jaune français: documents diplomatiques 1938–1939* (Paris, 1939), p. 312, Coulondre to Bonnet, 25 August 1939.

47. *Pravda*, 2 September 1939, p. 1. The paper reported Molotov's remark about the 'false games' played by the West, 'that Atlantic and French politicians tried to push the Soviet and German people away from one another'. On the ratification of the pact see G. Roberts, *Stalin's Wars: From World War to Cold War* (New Haven, Conn., 2006), pp. 33–5.

48. NA, PREM 1/331a, William Strang to Cadogan, 26 August 1939, p. 1. According to Hitler's adjutant, Major Engel, it was the Italian news that left him 'extremely bowled over', but Engel was only witness to the mood, not the events. See H. von Kotze (ed.), *Heeresadjutant bei Hitler 1938–1945: Aufzeichnungen des Majors Engel* (Stuttgart, 1974), p. 59.

49. Halifax papers, A4.4 10.3/10 (i), Birger Dahlerus, 'Report on Negotiations between Great Britain and Germany, Aug 24 until Sept 3 1939' [n.d. but December 1942], p. 11.

50. Butler papers, G10, draft notes, 'September 1939', p. 1.

51. Halifax papers, A4.4 10.3/12, 'Agreement between the Government of the United Kingdom and the Polish Government regarding Mutual Assistance', 25 August 1939, pp. 2, 4; A4.4 10.3/10, Halifax, 'A Record of Events before the War, 1939', p. 2.

52. Below, *At Hitler's Side*, p. 29; Fröhlich (ed.), *Tagebücher von Joseph Goebbels*, Band 7, p. 78, entry for 26 August 1939.

53. I. Kershaw, *Hitler: Nemesis 1936–1945* (London, 2000), p. 215.

54. Rohde et al., *Das Deutsche Reich und der Zweite Weltkrieg*, Band II, p. 87

55. Kotze, *Heeresadjutant bei Hitler*, p. 59, entry for 29 August 1939.

56. NA, PREM 1/331a, R. Makins (Foreign Office), 'Report of Conversation with M Burckhardt, 12 June 1939', p. 11; 'Summary of Comments' for the prime minister, 13 August 1939.

57. N. Nicolson (ed.), *Harold Nicolson: Diaries and Letters 1930–1939* (London, 1966), pp. 414–15.

58. Hore-Belisha papers, HOBE 5/67, Chatfield to Hore-Belisha, 26 August 1939. It is not clear that the West knew about the cancellation order. Chamberlain later assumed that it must have been the case. See Self (ed.), *Neville Chamberlain Diary Letters*, Vol. 4, p. 444, Neville Chamberlain to Ida Chamberlain, 10 September 1939.

59. Halifax papers, A4.410.3/10 (ii), 'Record of Events before the War', pp. 2–3; on the three principles insisted on, see A4.410.3/10 (i), Halifax to Cadogan, 29 April 1943 ('we harped on one theme,' remarked Halifax).

60. *Daily Telegraph*, 26 August 1939.

61. NA, PREM 1/331a, Strand to Cadogan, 26 August 1939, p. 3.

POLAND IN THE MIDDLE: 27–31 AUGUST

1. NA, PREM 1/331a, draft reply to message for the German chancellor, 27 August 1939; Sir John Simon, comments on draft, 27 August 1939.

2. Hore-Belisha papers, HOBE 5/67, rough notes for cabinet, 27 August 1939; Hore-Belisha to Sir John Simon, 27 August 1939.

3. Butler papers, G10, 'September 1939' [n.d.], p. 2.

4. Boyer de Sainte-Suzanne, *Une politique étrangère*, p. 72, entry for 27 August 1939.

5. Ibid., pp. 72–3, entries for 28, 29 August 1939. The French reads *'en risquant la guerre rouge, la guerre restera blanche'*.

6. J. Puyaubert, *Georges Bonnet: Les combats d'un pacifiste* (Rennes, 2007), pp. 239–41.

7. Rohde et al., *Das Deutsche Reich und der Zweite Weltkrieg*, Band II, pp. 103–4.

8. Hore-Belisha papers, 5/65, 'Precautionary Measures taken by the War Office', 22–28 August 1939.

9. NA, HO 45/18128, M. Bennett (Office of Works) to S. Baker (Home Office), 18 April 1939; letter from Bennett to R. Wells (Home Office), 31 August 1939.

10. Ibid., file 'Action to Protect Art Treasures, 1939'.

11. See D. Kaiser and T. W. Mason, 'Germany, "Domestic Crisis" and War: a Comment', and R. J. Overy, 'Reply', in *Past & Present*, 122 (1989), pp. 200–205, 205–21, 221–40.

12. Halifax papers, A4.410.3/10 (iii), 'Record of Events before the War', p. 3; Andrew, *Secret Service*, pp. 427–30.

13. Andrew, *Secret Service*, p. 430.

14. There is a vast literature on the German resistance and the coming of war. For a useful survey see T. Hamerow, *On the Road to the Wolf's Lair: German Resistance to Hitler* (Cambridge, Mass., 1997), pp. 248–57. On the links with foreign policy see D. Dilks, 'Determinanten britischer Deutschlandspolitik 1937–1939. Zum Stellenwert des Widerstandes in der britischen Politik', and K. von Klemperer, 'Die "Aussenpolitik" des deutschen Widerstandes', both in K-J. Müller and D. Dilks (eds.), *Grossbritannien und der deutsche Widerstand 1933–1944* (Paderborn, 1994), pp. 31–52, 83–94.

15. H. Gisevius, *To the Bitter End* (London, 1948), pp. 355–6.

16. U. von Hassell, *Die Hassell-Tagebücher 1938–1944* (Berlin, 1988), p. 112, entry for 26 August 1939.

17. Gisevius, *To the Bitter End*, pp. 369–70.

18. Ibid., p. 372.

19. NA, PREM 1/331a, minute for the prime minister, by Frederick Ashton Gwatkin, 27 August 1939.

20. Churchill College Archive, Christie papers, CHRS 1/29B, Christie to Vansittart, 29 August 1939.

21. Andrew, *Secret Service*, p. 430.

22. Halifax papers, A4.410.3/10 (i), Dahlerus, 'Report on Negotiations', p. 9; A4.410.3/10 (iii), Halifax, 'Record of Events before the War', p. 2.

23. Halifax papers A4.410.3/10 (i), 'Report on Negotiations', p. 14.

24. Butler papers, G10, notes 'September 1939', p. 3; Rhodes James (ed.), '*Chips*', p. 210, entry for 28 August 1939.

25. Halifax papers, A4.410.3/10 (i), notes by Frank Roberts on Dahlerus manuscript, December 1942.

26. On Göring's role see S. Martens, *Hermann Göring: 'Erste Paladin des Führers' und 'zweiter Mann im Reich'* (Paderborn, 1985), pp. 193–5, 199–200.

27. Andrew, *Secret Service*, p. 430. On the appointment of the Reich Defence Council see *Dokumente der Deutschen Politik: 1939*, Band I (Berlin, 1941) pp. 393–4, 'Erlass über die Bildung eines Ministerrats für die Reichsverteidigung', 30 August 1939.

28. Hartman, *Halder*, p. 137.

29. Engelmann, *In Hitler's Germany*, pp. 150–51.

30. Kotze, *Heeresadjutant bei Hitler*, p. 60, entry for 29 August 1939.

31. Fröhlich (ed.), *Tagebücher von Joseph Goebbels*, Band 7, pp. 80–81, entry for 28 August 1939.

32. Jędrzejewicz (ed.), *Diplomat in Berlin*, pp. 600–601.

33. M. Domarus, *Hitler: Reden und Proklamationen 1932–1945*, Band II (1): *Untergang* (Munich, 1965), pp. 1296.

34. NA, PREM 1/331a, Nevile Henderson to Horace Wilson,

9 May 1939, p. 1; on Henderson's embassy in Berlin see P. Neville, 'The Appointment of Sir Nevile Henderson, 1937 – Design or Blunder?', *Journal of Contemporary History*, 33 (1998), pp. 609–19.

35. NA, PREM 1/331a, Henderson to Halifax, 16 August 1939.

36. Henderson, *Failure of a Mission*, p. 263.

37. Boyer de Sainte-Suzanne, *Une politique étrangère*, p. 73, entry for 29 August 1939.

38. Halifax papers, A4.410.3/10 (iii), 'Record of Events before the War', p. 3; Hill (ed.), *Die Weizsäcker-Papiere*, p. 162, entry for 29 August 1939; D. Dilks (ed.), *The Diaries of Sir Alexander Cadogan* (London, 1971), p. 204.

39. Henderson, *Failure of a Mission*, p. 264.

40. Dilks (ed.), *Diaries of Sir Alexander Cadogan*, p. 205, entry for 30 August 1939. See too Halifax papers, A4.410.3/10 (iii), 'Record of Events before the War', p. 3; A4.410.3/10(i), Notes by Halifax for E. L. Woodward, 10 December 1942, which explain why Göring's intervention was seen as 'unacceptable': 'Germany did not regard the Poles as a "desirable nation" and did not consider Poland a British interest.'

41. NA, PREM 1/331a, note for Cadogan from Halifax [n.d.]; Hore-Belisha to Halifax, 30 August 1939.

42. Dilks (ed.), *Diaries of Sir Alexander Cadogan*, p. 205, entry for 30 August 1939; Domarus, *Hitler: Reden und Proklamationen*, Band II (1), p. 1294, who reports Göring's response as 'Nonsense, negotiations must take place in Berlin.'

43. P. Schmidt, *Statist auf diplomatische Bühne* (Bonn, 1949), p. 457.

44. Ibid., p. 458.

45. J. von Ribbentrop, *The Ribbentrop Memoirs* (London, 1954), p. 123; Schmidt, *Statist*, p. 459.

46. Henderson, *Failure of a Mission*, p. 273.

47. Jędrzejewicz (ed.), *Diplomat in Berlin*, pp. 608–10.

48. Rhodes James (ed.), '*Chips*', p. 211, entry for 30 August 1939.

49. Spears, *Assignment to Catastrophe*, p. 26; J. Barnes and D. Nicholson (eds.), *The Empire at Bay: The Leo Amery Diaries 1929–1945* (London, 1988), p. 569, entry for 30 August 1939.

50. Nicolson (ed.), *Harold Nicolson*, pp. 414–15, entries for 29, 30 August 1939. Nicolson observed that the stock market actually went up as a result of the changed mood.

51. D. Sheridan (ed.), *Wartime Women: A Mass Observation Anthology, 1937–1945* (London, 1990), p. 50.

52. A. Maurois, *Memoirs 1885–1967* (London, 1970), pp. 210–11.

53. Ibid., pp. 209–10.

54. Puyaubert, *Georges Bonnet*, pp. 203–5; Bonnet, *Quai d'Orsay*, pp. 258–9; E. du Réau, *Édouard Daladier 1884–1970* (Paris, 1993), pp. 362–3. On the popular mood in favour of firmness see J.-L. Crémieux-Brilhac, *Les Français de l'an 40: La guerre oui ou non?* (Paris, 1990), pp. 63–5; D. Hucker, 'French Public Attitudes Towards the Prospect of War in 1938–39: "Pacifism" or "War Anxiety"?', *French History*, 21 (2007), pp. 431–49.

55. H. Krausnick and H. H. Wilhelm, *Die Truppe des Weltanschauungskrieges: Die Einsatzgruppen der Sicherheits-polizei und des SD 1938–1942* (Stuttgart, 1981), pp. 33–4, 36–7.

56. E. B. Westermann, *Hitler's Police Battalions: Enforcing Racial War in the East* (Lawrence, Kan., 2005), pp. 124–8.

57. On the development of these fantasies see H. Schaller, *Der Nationalsozialismus und die slawische Welt* (Regensburg, 2002).

58. Domarus, *Hitler: Reden und Proklamationen*, Band II (1),

p. 1289; Below, *At Hitler's Side*, p. 30, entry for 30 August 1939.

59. Imperial War Museum, London, Nuremberg trial papers, Case XI, doc. Book 1b, Fritzsche affidavit, 29 June 1948.

60. Fröhlich (ed.), *Tagebücher von Joseph Goebbels*, Band 7, p. 87, entry for 1 September 1939.

61. Domarus, *Hitler: Reden und Proklamationen*, Band II (1), pp. 1299–300, Weisung Nr 1 für die Kriegführung; Hill (ed.), *Die Weizsäcker-Papiere*, p. 164, entry for 7 September 1939; Hartman, *Halder*, p. 139.

62. G. Meyer (ed.), *Generalfeldmarschall Wilhelm Ritter von Leeb: Tagesbuchaufzeichnungen und Lagebeurteilung aus zwei Weltkriegen* (Stuttgart, 1976), pp. 170–71, entries for 31 August, 2 September 1939.

63. M. R. Dederichs, *Heydrich: The Face of Evil* (London, 2006), p. 89; W. Schellenberg, *The Schellenberg Memoirs* (London, 1956), pp. 68–70.

LOCAL WAR OR WORLD WAR?: 1–3 SEPTEMBER

1. Schenk, *Hitlers Mann in Danzig*, pp. 127–9; Levine, *Hitler's Free City*, pp. 152–3.

2. Klukowski, *Diary from the Years of Occupation*, p. 5, entry for 1 September 1939.

3. H. Eberle and M. Uhl (eds.), *The Hitler Book: The Secret Dossier Prepared for Stalin* (London, 2005), pp. 46–7; Domarus, *Hitler: Reden und Proklamationen*, Band II (1), pp. 1310–11.

4. *Dokumente der Deutschen Politik, 1939*, Band I, pp. 256–7, Reichstagsrede des Führers, 1 September 1939.

5. Eberle and Uhl (eds.), *The Hitler Book*, p. 47; Fröhlich (ed.), *Tagebücher von Joseph Goebbels*, Band 7, p. 89, entry for 2 September 1939.

6. *Dokumente der Deutschen Politik, 1939*, Band II, pp. 596–7, Gesetz über die Wiedervereinigung der Freien Stadt Danzig mit dem Deutschen Reich, 1 September 1939; Eberle and Uhl (eds.), *The Hitler Book*, p. 47.

7. M. Moll (ed.), *'Führe-Erlasse' 1939–1945* (Stuttgart, 1997), p. 193, 'Euthanasiebefehl'.

8. NA, PREM 1/331a, telegram to prime minister, 1 September 1939; Halifax papers, A4.410.3/10 (iii), 'Record of Events before the War', pp. 3–4.

9. Hore-Belisha papers, HOBE 1/8, diary 1939, entry for 1 September 1939. The phrase is missing from the published diary. See R. J. Minney (ed.), *The Private Papers of Hore-Belisha* (London, 1960), p. 225.

10. NA, PREM 1/331a, note for prime minister, 31 August 1939.

11. Reynaud, *La France a sauvé l'Europe*, Vol. 1, p. 598; Halifax papers, A4.410.3/10 (iii), 'Record of Events before the War', p. 4.

12. President's Secretary's Files. Box 47, Note, 1 Sept 1939 (initialled by Roosevelt).

13. Minney (ed.), *Private Papers of Hore-Belisha*, p. 225; NA, AIR 8/266, Ismay to Newall, 1 September 1939.

14. NA, AIR 8/266, Air Ministry to air officers commanderin-chief, 1 September 1939.

15. NA, PREM 1/331a, draft statement on Poland, 1 September 1939.

16. Nicolson (ed.); *Harold Nicolson*, pp. 416–17, entry for 1 September 1939.

17. *Parliamentary Debates*, Vol. 351, col. 131, 1 September 1939.

18. Boyer de Sainte-Suzanne, *Une politique étrangère*, p. 75, entry for 1 September 1939.

19. Reynaud, *La France a sauvé l'Europe*, Vol. 1, p. 599; Cmd 6106, 'Documents concerning German–Polish Relations', p. 169, Henderson to Halifax, 1 September 1939; *Le Livre jaune français*, p. 389, Coulondre to Bonnet, 1 September 1939.

20. Eberle and Uhl (eds.), *The Hitler Book*, p. 47.

21. Halifax papers, A4.410.3/10 (iii), 'Record of Events before the War', p. 4; Henderson, *Failure of a Mission*, p. 279.

22. Shirer, *Berlin Diary*, p. 160, entry for 1 September 1939; Fröhlich (ed.), *Tagebücher von Joseph Goebbels*, Band 7, p. 89, entry for 2 September 1939.

23. V. Klemperer, *I Shall Bear Witness: The Diaries of Victor Klemperer 1933–41* (London, 1998), p. 294, entry for 1 September 1939.

24. M. Muggeridge *The Thirties: 1930–1940 in Great Britain* (London, 1940), p. 310.

25. Rhodes James (ed.), '*Chips*', p. 211, entry for 1 September 1939.

26. Nicolson (ed.), *Harold Nicolson*, p. 418, entry for 1 September 1939.

27. Spears, *Assignment to Catastrophe*, p. 78; H. Macmillan, *Winds of Change 1914–1939* (London, 1966), p. 605.

28. NA, PREM 1/331a, note on French negotiations, 2/3 September 1939; telegram from Phipps (Paris) to Foreign Office, 2 September 1939. See too Réau, *Édouard Daladier*, pp. 363–5.

29. NA, PREM 1/331a, Foreign Office minute, 27 August 1939.

30. De Felice (ed.), *Galeazzo Ciano*, pp. 338–9, entry for 31 August 1939.

31. R. De Felice, *Mussolini il duce*, Vol. II: *Lo stato totalitario, 1936–1940* (Turin, 1981), pp. 670–71.

32. Puyaubert, *Georges Bonnet*, pp. 203–4, 206; Halifax papers, A4.410.3/10 (iii), 'Record of Events before the War', p. 3.

33. Bonnet, *Quai d'Orsay*, pp. 261–2.

34. NA, PREM 1/331a, note for the prime minister, 2 September 1939. See too J. Bardoux, *Journal d'un Témoin de la Troisième* (Paris, 1957), p. 75, for the constitutional arguments between Bonnet and Daladier.

35. Fröhlich (ed.), *Tagebücher von Joseph Goebbels*, Band 7, pp. 90–91, entry for 3 September 1939.

36. Churchill College Archive, Phipps papers, PHPP 5/8, Chamberlain to Daladier, 13 July 1939; NA, PREM 1/331a, minute for the prime minister, 12 August 1939: 'It is also reported that Mussolini intends to intervene late in a crisis with a proposal for a conference.'

37. Bonnet, *Quai d'Orsay*, pp. 264–5; NA, PREM 1/331a, note on Italian proposals, 2 September 1939.

38. NA, PREM 1/331a, draft note on Italian proposals, 2 September 1939; Foreign Office minute on Ciano's proposal, 2 September 1939.

39. De Felice (ed.), *Galeazzo Ciano*, p. 341; NA, PREM 1/331a, Foreign Office minute on Ciano's proposals, 2 September 1939, p. 1.

40. G. Pini, *Filo diretto con Palazzo Venezia* (Bologna, 1950), p. 196.

41. Cited in G. De Luna, 'L'identità coatta. Gli italiani in Guerra (1940–1945)', in W. Barberis (ed.) *Guerra e Pace*, Annali 18 (Turin, 2002), p. 758.

42. *I documenti diplomatici italiani, 8 ser. 1935–39* (Rome, 1953), xiii, p. 385, Hitler to Mussolini, 3 September 1939.

43. *Il Popolo d'Italia*, 5 September 1939.

44. A. Briggs, *The History of Broadcasting in the United*

Kingdom, Vol. II: *The Golden Age of Wireless* (Oxford, 1965), p. 659.

45. Halifax papers, A4.410.3/10 (iii), 'Record of Events before the War', pp. 4–5.

46. Hore-Belisha papers, HOBE 1/8, Diary 1939, entry for 2 September 1939.

47. Spears, *Assignment to Catastrophe*, p. 30.

48. Nicolson (ed.), *Harold Nicolson*, p. 418, entry for 2 September 1939.

49. *Parliamentary Debates*, Vol. 351, cols. 281–2, 2 September 1939.

50. Spears, *Assignment to Catastrophe*, p. 31.

51. Barnes and Nicholson (eds.), *The Leo Amery Diaries*, p. 370; Nicolson (ed.), *Harold Nicolson*, p. 419.

52. *Parliamentary Debates*, vol. 351, cols., 282–6; G. Brown *Maxton* (Edinburgh, 1986), p. 297.

53. Barnes and Nicholson (eds.), *Empire at Bay*, p. 570.

54. D. Dutton, *Simon: A Political Biography of Sir John Simon* (London, 1992), pp. 280–81; Halifax papers, A4.410.3/10 (iii), 'Record of Events before the War', p. 5.

55. Dutton, *Simon*, pp. 281–2; Halifax papers, A4.410.3/10 (iii), 'Record of Events before the War', p. 5.

56. Halifax papers, A4.410.3/10 (iii), 'Record of Events before the War', p. 5.

57. Phipps papers, PHPP I 2/1, Cadogan to Phipps, 6 September 1939.

58. Self (ed.), *Neville Chamberlain Diary Letters*, Vol. 4, p. 443, Neville Chamberlain to Ida Chamberlain, 10 September 1939.

59. Nicolson (ed.), *Harold Nicolson*, p. 417, entry for 1 September 1939.

60. *Le Livre jaune français*, pp. 397–404, 'Déclaration lue le

2 septembre 1939 par M. Daladier'.

61. Bardoux, *Journal d'un Témoin*, p. 76.

62. Boyer de Sainte-Suzanne, *Une politique étrangère*, p. 76, entry for 2 September 1939; Puyaubert, *Georges Bonnet*, pp. 213–14.

THE FAILURE OF PEACE: 3 SEPTEMBER 1939

1. S. Jameson, *Journey from the North: Autobiography of Storm Jameson* (2 vols., London, 1969–70), Vol. 2, p. 27.

2. Halifax papers, A4.410.3/10 (iii), 'Record of Events before the War', p. 6.

3. Ibid., p. 6; Dilks (ed.), *Diaries of Sir Alexander Cadogan*, p. 213, entry for 3 September 1939.

4. Halifax papers, A4.410.3/10 (iii), 'Record of Events before the War', p. 6; Cadogan papers, ACAD 1/8, Diary 1939, entry for 3 September 1939.

5. NA, CAB 127/158, Horace Wilson papers, 'Munich 1938', p. 58.

6. Butler papers, G10, text of prime minister's broadcast, 3 September 1939.

7. Butler papers, G10, notes on 'September 1939' [n.d.], p. 4.

8. Dilks (ed.), *Diaries of Sir Alexander Cadogan*, p. 213, entry for 3 September 1939; Nicolson (ed.), *Harold Nicolson*, p. 422, entry for 3 September 1939; J. Kennedy, *The Business of War: The War Narrative of Major-General Sir John Kennedy* (London, 1957), p. 16.

9. Barnes and Nicholson (eds.), *The Empire at Bay*, p. 571, entry for 3 September 1939.

10. N. Mackenzie and J. Mackenzie (eds.), *The Diaries of*

Beatrice Webb (London, 2000), p. 570, entry for 3 September 1939.

11. P. Mortimer, *About Time, 1918–1939* (London, 1979), p. 189.

12. Somerville College, Oxford, Vera Brittain papers, Archive D, diary, 1 September 1939, p. 5; 3 September 1939, p. 6.

13. NA, CAB 127/158, Horace Wilson, 'Munich 1938', pp. 158–9.

14. Self (ed.), *Neville Chamberlain Diary Letters*, Vol. 4, pp. 443–4, letter to Ida Chamberlain, 10 September 1939.

15. Spears, *Assignment to Catastrophe*, p. 36; Rhodes James (ed.), *'Chips'*, p. 215, entry for 3 September 1939.

16. *Parliamentary Debates*, Vol. 351, col. 298, 3 September 1939.

17. Schmidt, *Statist*, p. 464. On the telegram to Hitler, see M. Bloch, *Ribbentrop* (London, 1992), pp. 259–60.

18. O. Dietrich, *The Hitler I Knew* (London, 1955), p. 47.

19. *Dokumente der Deutschen Politik, 1939*, Band I, pp. 269–73, Memorandum der deutschen Regierung, 3 September 1939; Fröhlich (ed.), *Tagebücher von Joseph Goebbels*, Band 7, pp. 91–2; Halifax papers, A4.410.3/10 (i), Dahlerus 'Report on Negotiations'.

20. Below, *At Hitler's Side*, p. 33; Frölich (ed.), *Tagebücher von Joseph Goebbels*, Band 7, p. 91, entry for 4 September 1939.

21. W. Warlimont, *Inside Hitler's Headquarters* (London, 1964), p. 32; Fröhlich (ed.), *Tagebücher von Joseph Goebbels*, Band 7, p. 92.

22. Speer, *Inside the Third Reich*, p. 167.

23. Halifax papers, A4.410.3/10 (i), Dahlerus, 'Report on Negotiations', p. 42.

24. Fröhlich (ed.), *Tagebücher von Joseph Goebbels*, Band 7, p. 92.

25. Shirer, *Berlin Diary*, pp. 161–2.

26. Puyaubert, *Georges Bonnet*, pp. 212–13.

27. Bonnet, *Quai d'Orsay*, p. 271–2.

28. Ibid., p. 265.

29. D. C. Watt, *How War Came: The Immediate Origins of the Second World War, 1938–1939* (London, 1989), pp. 598–60; *Livre jaune francais*, pp. 412–13, Coulondre to Bonnet, 3 September 1939.

30. Boyer de Sainte-Suzanne, *Une politique étrangère*, pp. 76–7.

31. Crémieux-Brilhac, *Les francais de l'an* 40, pp. 57–8; Bardoux, *Journal d'un Témoin*, p. 78.

32. Maurois, *Memoirs*, p. 211.

33. *Le Livre jaune francais*, pp. 415–16, É. Daladier, Appel à la nation, 3 September 1939. See too Hucker, 'French public attitudes', p. 448.

34. A. Jackson, *The British Empire and the Second World War* (London, 2006), pp. 19–20; on French imperial preparations see C. Levisse-Touze, 'La préparation économique, industrielle et militaire de l'Afrique du Nord à la veille de la guerre', *Revue d'histoire de la deuxième guerre mondiale*, 36 (1986), pp. 2–5.

35. Klukowski, *Diary from the Years of Occupation*, p. 6, entry for 4 September 1939.

36. Léon Noël, *Une ambassade a Varsovie 1935–1939* (Paris, 1946), p. 488.

37. Warlimont, *Inside Hitler's Headquarters*, p. 31; Domarus, *Hitler: Reden und Proklamationen*, Band II (1), pp. 1344–5, Weisung Nr 2 für die Kriegführung.

38. *Fuehrer Conferences on Naval Affairs, 1939–1945* (London, 1990), pp. 37–8, 'Reflections of the C-in-C, Navy, on the outbreak of war', 3 September 1939.

39. Kennedy, *Business of War*, p. 16.

40. R. Macleod and D. Kelly (eds.), *The Ironside Diaries, 1937–1940* (London, 1962), pp. 92–4, entry for 3 September 1939; Hore-Belisha papers, 1/7, diary typescript, 3 September 1939.

41. Rohde et al., *Das Deutsche Reich und der Zweite Weltkrieg*, Band 2, pp. 103–6.

42. Hankey papers, 10/2, Robin Hankey to Maurice Hankey, 5 September 1939.

43. Hankey papers, 4/31, notes for a speech [n.d. but September 1939], p. 4.

44. Hankey papers, 10/1, 'Britain's Acceptance', 1 September 1939, published in *The Times* of 2 September 1939.

45. NA, AIR/8 266, Air Ministry to C-in-C, Bomber, Coastal and Fighter Commands, 3 September 1939; Air Ministry minute, 'Emergency measures taken to mid-day', 3 September 1939.

46. *Fuehrer Conferences on Naval Affairs*, p. 39. The information was taken from the interrogation of Admiral Godt, Dönitz's chief of staff in autumn 1939.

47. Muggeridge, *The Thirties*, p. 310.

48. Cadogan papers, 1/8, diary, 3 September 1939. The reference to the guided tour he gave to his wife is absent from the published diary.

49. Bradford, *King George VI*, p. 304.

50. Puyaubert, *Georges Bonnet*, p. 214.

51. D. Sheridan (ed.), *Wartime Women: A Mass Observation Anthology 1937–1945* (London, 2000), p. 56.

52. Berle papers, Box 64, draft Presidential Radio Message, 3 Sept 1939, p. 2; B. B. Berle, T. B. Jacobs (eds), *Navigating the Rapids 1918–1971: From the Papers of Adolf A. Berle* (New York, 1973), p. 248.

53. *Dokumente der deutschen Politik*, 1939, Band I, pp. 397–8,

Verordnung über ausserordentlicher Rundfunkmassnahmen, 1 September 1939.

54. Hartman, *Halder*, p. 142.

55. Hill (ed.), *Die Weizsäcker-Papiere*, p. 164, entry for 5 September 1939.

56. Halifax papers, A4.410.3/10 (i), Dahlerus, 'Report on Negotiations', pp. 42, 44.

CONCLUSION: WHY WAR?

1. 'Documents concerning German–Polish Relations', p. 97, letter from the prime minister to the German chancellor, 22 August 1939.

2. Halifax papers, A4.410.12/1, draft note 'Foreign Policy 1938–9' [n.d.], p. 2.

3. Halifax papers, A4.410.3/10 (ii), letter from Woodward to Halifax, 11 September 1943; letter Cadogan to Halifax, 16 April 1943.

4. Ibid., Woodward to Halifax, 11 September 1943, encl. proof copy and Halifax's comments, pp. 2–3.

5. See especially M. Mazower, *Hitler's Empire: Nazi Rule in Occupied Europe* (London, 2008). See too Schaller, *Der Nationalsozialismus und die slawische Welt*, pp. 175–86.

6. A. Tooze, *The Wages of Destruction: The Making and Breaking of the Nazi Economy* (London, 2006), pp. 322, 323–4.

7. Ibid., pp. 324–5; on the turn to the West see too G. Weinberg, *Hitler's Foreign Policy, 1937–1939* (Chicago, 1980).

8. See E. Syring *Hitler: seine politische Utopie* (Berlin, 1994), esp. pp. 218–37, for the turn to the East.

9. *Hitlers politisches Testament. Die Bormann-Diktate vom Februar und April 1945* (Hamburg, 1981), pp. 1–2.

10. Speer, *Inside the Third Reich*, p. 165. Speer had first elaborated these views under interrogation in Germany in the summer of 1945: 'I do not think this was the time when Hitler wanted a large-scale conflict. On the whole, I don't think Hitler wanted a conflict with the Western powers.' See R. J. Overy, *Interrogations: The Nazi Elite in Allied Hands, 1945* (London, 2001), p. 331.

11. Below, *At Hitler's Side*, p. 32.

12. P. J. Buchanan, *Churchill, Hitler and the Unnecessary War: How Britain Lost its Empire and the West Lost the World* (New York, 2008), pp. 266–7, 271, 293.

13. Dilks (ed.), *Diaries of Sir Alexander Cadogan*, p. 206, entry for 31 August 1939.

14. Butler papers, F80, memorandum by Oliver Harvey, 6 April 1939, p. 10.

15. Halifax papers, A4.410.1/2, speech at Ashridge, 24 February 1939, p. 24d.

16. Halifax papers, A4.410.1/4, notes for a speech at Leeds, 20 January 1940, p. 1.

17. Sheridan (ed.), *Wartime Women*, p. 46.

18. Butler papers, G10, Duke of Buccleuch to Butler, 25 July 1939.

19. NA, PREM 1/393, file 'Anglo-French declaration of War Aims', November 1939.

20. Maurois, *Memoirs*, p. 209.

21 Speer, *Inside the Third Reich*, pp. 164–5.

22. Fröhlich (ed.), *Tagebücher von Joseph Goebbels*, Band 7, 74, 78, entries for 23 August, 26 August.

23. Dilks (ed.), *Diaries of Sir Alexander Cadogan*, pp. 205–6, entries for 30 August, 31 August.

24. Self (ed.), *Neville Chamberlain Diary Letters*, Vol. 4, pp. 440–41, letter from Neville Chamberlain to Hilda Chamberlain, 27 August 1939.

25. NA, PREM 1/ 312, Lord Chatfield to Chamberlain, 30 August 1939.

26. Butler papers, G10, rough notes 'Position of British Policy' [end August 1939].

27. *Parliamentary Debates*, Vol. 351, col. 283, 2 September 1939.

28. Reynaud, *La France a sauvé l'Europe*, Vol. 1, p. 590.

29. Phipps papers, PHPP I 1/23, letter from Phipps to Halifax, 25 September 1939.

Index